The Making and Remaking of the British Constitution

Law in its Social Setting

The Making and Remaking of the British Constitution

The Radcliffe Lectures at the University of Warwick for 1996–97 as delivered by

Rt Hon Lord Nolan of Brasted

and

Sir Stephen Sedley

with a Postscript by

Professor Geoffrey Wilson

BLACKSTONE
PRESS LIMITED

First published in Great Britain 1997 by Blackstone Press Limited, Aldine Place, London W12 8AA.   Telephone: 0181-740 2277

© Legal Research Institute 1997

ISBN: 1 85431 704 0

British Library Cataloguing in Publication Data
A CIP catalogue record for this book is available from the British Library.

Typeset by Montage Studios Limited, Tonbridge, Kent
Printed by Bell & Bain Limited, Glasgow

Contents

Preface

The Radcliffe lectures are an annual series of lectures given at the University of Warwick. They commemorate the name of Lord Radcliffe, the first Chancellor of the University. The practice has been for different schools and departments in the University to act as hosts and presenters. In the 1996–97 academic year it was the Law School's turn and it invited Lord Nolan and Sir Stephen Sedley to share the lectures between them.

The subject they chose was 'The Making and Remaking of the British Constitution' and they delivered the lectures in alternate weeks in November and December 1996. The Law School is very grateful to them for sparing the time which often involved lengthy travel at the end of busy days, in the case of Lord Nolan from his work on his Committee on Standards in Public Life, and for Sir Stephen Sedley from his work as a High Court judge on circuit, which he combines with his work as a judge dealing with administrative law matters in the Queen's Bench Division of the High Court. The lectures were well received at the time and commented upon in the national press and it seemed appropriate to make them available to a wider audience. They are printed in the order in which they were delivered, together with a postscript by Professor Geoffrey Wilson who chaired the lectures.

Professor Mike McConville
School of Law, University of Warwick
July 1997

Table of Cases

Table of Statutes

1. General Introduction

Rt Hon Lord Nolan

In these three Radcliffe lectures I shall speak about the three major arms of the British constitution — the legislature, the executive and the judiciary. My co-lecturer, Stephen Sedley, is considering in some detail the relationship between the judiciary and the other branches. So to some extent we are covering similar ground. In my lectures, therefore, I shall seek to approach the topic from a standpoint which is not specifically that of the law, but rather that of an observer of the constitution as it functions in practice.

It is appropriate for me to take this approach, because in the last two years my name has been particularly associated with the Chairmanship of the Committee on Standards in Public Life, a committee which through no fault of its own has become colloquially known as the Nolan Committee. This is not a judicial committee, but a body which resembles the traditional Royal Commission, though with the important difference that its members were appointed for a period of three years as a standing (though by no means static) committee.

I am also the Commissioner for the Interception of Communications — a statutory role in which as a senior judge I am invited to act as a formal and continuing scrutineer of the actions of the executive in a particular area of its work. I fulfil these two roles, as Chairman and Commissioner, alongside my responsibilities as a Law Lord, in which capacity I am a member of both the judiciary and the legislature.

I mention these roles for two reasons. Firstly Lord Radcliffe, a man for whose abilities and intellect I had enormous respect, demonstrated the contribution which judges in this country have often been asked to make to the body politic. Radcliffe chaired Commission after Commission, to the extent that A. P. Herbert was able to coin his famous phrase of the time 'government by Radcliffery'. Indeed he also performed a direct role in the executive when, during the war, he interrupted his career at the Bar to become Director-General — in effect Permanent Secretary — of the Ministry of Information.

Secondly, these lectures take place against the background of a debate about the proper role of the judiciary, and the raising of questions as to whether judges are overstepping the boundaries of their constitutional position. An important aspect is of course the development of administrative law, and the growth of judicial review. But the issues go wider than that, and touch on the rights of judges, for example, to comment on questions of public policy.

These are points which both Stephen Sedley and I consider in our lectures. But Cyril Radcliffe did not appoint himself half a century ago to the first of his Commissions, or to any of the others on which he served over the next thirty years. And I did not appoint myself. We were appointed on each occasion by the government of the day. Often, as with the Nolan Committee, the appointment was made with the support of the opposition party leaders in Parliament.

Law Lords, I might add, are appointed by the Queen on the recommendation of the prime minister. So are judges of the Court of Appeal. In both cases the prime minister acts with the help of advice from the Lord Chancellor, but it is the prime minister who selects the appointees. The Lord Chancellor is responsible for recommending or making appointments to the High Court and the courts below. It is, of course, the Lord Chancellor who not only embodies the law but combines in his office each of the three elements of the constitution.

Thus the separation of powers in this country has never been as absolute as in the United States of America. Ministers — the executive — serve in the legislature, as do senior judges. Judges undertake tasks for the executive, and on occasion for the legislature.

The ancient notion of the 'High Court of Parliament' survives to the extent that the House of Commons, though not a court of record, retains judicial and punitive powers in cases of contempt. The House of Lords is, of course, a court of record, and retains its role as the final court of appeal in the United Kingdom. Appeals are heard by Appellate Committees composed of Law Lords, but the decision in each case is that of the House as a whole and is given in the Chamber. It is only by convention that peers other than the Law Lords do not speak or vote upon the motion to allow or dismiss the particular appeal. Finally, the executive through subordinate legislation has considerable legislative powers subject only to minimal Parliamentary scrutiny.

My three lectures need to be seen against that background, in which the roles of the various arms of the constitution change over time, and where functions which may be seen historically as the preserve of one arm may unobtrusively and gradually pass to another.

THE LEGISLATURE

In this first lecture I want to discuss the role of the legislature. I shall identify three strands of development which have led to uncertainty about the role of Parliament, and offer some thoughts about future directions. I have called the strands 'sovereignty and influence', 'control of the executive', and 'public standing and perception'.

Sovereignty and Influence

I have had in my possession since I was a student a book published half a century ago — the 1946 edition of Wade and Phillips on *Constitutional Law*. An entire section of the book is devoted to the 'British Empire and Commonwealth'. This sentence appears in its opening paragraph:

> The Parliament of the United Kingdom has imperial functions and, as the Imperial Parliament, exercises legislative supremacy over British India and the Colonies and has a special relationship with the self-governing Dominions.

Only a few months after that volume was published, Cyril Radcliffe played an important part in dismantling that empire, when he chaired the Commission which hastily drew up the borders of the new independent India and Pakistan. A quarter of a century ago, in 1972, Parliament passed the European Communities Act.

The consequences of the Act were not, I think, widely understood by the general public at the time but were swiftly recognised and put into effect by the courts in a number of decisions during the middle and late 1970s. For example, in *Macarthys Ltd* v *Smith* [1979] 3 All ER 325, 329, after summarising the issues in the case, Lord Denning said:

> If on close investigation it should appear that our legislation is deficient or is inconsistent with Community law by some oversight of our draftsmen then it is our bounden duty to give priority to Community law. Such is the result of section 2(1) and (4) of the European Communities Act 1972.

Lord Denning continued in these terms:

> I pause here, however, to make one observation on a constitutional point. Thus far I have assumed that our Parliament, whenever it passes legislation, intends to fulfil its obligations under the Treaty. If the time

should come when our Parliament deliberately passes an Act with the intention of repudiating the Treaty or any provision in it or intentionally of acting inconsistently with it and says so in express terms then I should have thought that it would be the duty of our courts to follow the statute of our Parliament. I do not, however, envisage any such situation.

In his judgment in *H. P. Bulmer Ltd* v *J. Bollinger SA* [1974] Ch 401, Lord Denning had already spoken of the Treaty as being 'like an incoming tide. It flows into the estuaries and up the rivers. It cannot be held back'.

The acceptance thus accorded to the introduction of supervening Community law has been dutifully maintained in the courts throughout the 1980s and 1990s. Relations between judges and other lawyers in the United Kingdom and on the Continent are closer and more friendly than they have ever been. The public mood has developed rather differently. And it came as something of a shock to those inside as well as outside the legal profession when in the *Factortame* case [1991] 1 AC 603 the House of Lords was, for the first time, required to ignore or 'dis-apply' a United Kingdom Act of Parliament, the Merchant Shipping Act 1988, in deciding how to deal with the case before it. This was no more than a consistent and logical development of the law as enacted in the European Communities Act 1972, as Lord Bridge in *Factortame* was at pains to make clear. He said, at pp. 658–9 of the report:

If the supremacy within the European Community of Community law over the national law of member states was not always inherent in the EEC Treaty it was certainly well established in the jurisprudence of the European Court of Justice long before the United Kingdom joined the Community. Thus, whatever limitation of its sovereignty Parliament accepted when it enacted the European Communities Act 1972 was entirely voluntary. Under the terms of the Act of 1972 it has always been clear that it was the duty of a United Kingdom court, when delivering final judgment, to override any rule of national law found to be in conflict with any directly enforceable rule of Community law.

But the practical result of the case, namely that the House of Lords granted an injunction to forbid a minister from obeying an Act of Parliament, was seen by many as a revolutionary development. It brought home the fact that the incoming tide of Community law was not merely lapping on to the Westminster terraces but submerging part of our statute law. It reinforced the anxieties of those who fear that the continuing development of the European Union could reduce Parliament to the status of an offshore regional assembly.

The decline from Imperial Parliament towards offshore regional assembly has of course been neither as rapid nor as clear-cut as the pessimists would have us believe. The beginning of the diminution of the Imperial powers of Parliament preceded the apogee of Empire — usually seen as Queen Victoria's Diamond Jubilee of 1897 — by over half a century. It dates from the Durham Report of 1839, which led to responsible government in the Dominions. In many ways, the Imperial Parliament was never truly an Imperial legislature, and the Empire can be seen more as an exercise in *Realpolitik* by the executive, which adapted governing structures to suit the needs of the particular territory and of the moment. At the other end of the scale, Parliament has not been reduced to the status of an offshore assembly, and will not reach that stage, so long as it retains the fundamental criterion of national sovereignty, which is the ultimate ability to repeal the 1972 Act and to withdraw from the Union, however unlikely this may seem in practice.

It is instructive to consider that twenty five years passed between the day the King lost the title of King-Emperor and the day when, after lengthy negotiations, we joined the European Community. It is forty years since Suez demonstrated that we had lost our independent role as a world power, and thirty five years since we first applied for membership of what was then the EEC. For the last thirty five years we have either been trying to join the European Community, or we have been members of it, and it has been our own choice. No one has made us do it. The decision to join, and to remain, was taken by the British government and Parliament supported by a referendum, because we considered it to be in our best interests. The option of leaving has been there all that time. When we subordinate domestic control over certain matters to Brussels decisions, it is as part of a package which we judge to be beneficial overall. Through all this, sovereignty in law ultimately remains with Parliament. However, the contrast which can be drawn between 1946 and 1996 forms one of the three strands of development which create uncertainty about the present-day role and status of Parliament.

Our traditional view of the Mother of Parliaments, moving ever onwards and upwards from the Magna Carta of 1215 and the first Parliament later in the same century and admired the world over, was part of a certain and comfortable view of our place in the scheme of things. The famous remark of Dean Acheson that 'Britain has lost an empire but has not yet found a role' was made over thirty years ago, but in many respects remains true today. It is particularly true of Parliament, that most conservative of institutions. British Foreign Secretaries still have to respond to Parliamentary questions which envisage a capacity to intervene in the affairs of other countries far beyond our actual capabilities, even though it may well be true, in a phrase often attributed to Douglas Hurd, that we 'punch above our weight'. But the problem of Parliamentary insecurity over its role in the world goes well beyond the occasional flight of fancy over foreign policy. Parliament is being squeezed from a number of directions. Europe is one. Ministers still have the power of veto over Brussels decisions, except where qualified majority voting has been conceded, but Parliament has not. It can only draw ministers' attention to aspects of draft Directives. It cannot block them, or force ministers to block them.

Parliament also feels squeezed from below. One of the consequences of greater stability within Western Europe is a reduction in the bonds of necessity which unite the nation state. There is no immediate external threat which makes tight national unity a priority. And there is a reaction against uniformity. So in Britain, as in other western European countries, there is a growing movement to build on those cultural and historic identities which were merged into the nation states of recent times. This emerges as nationalism, or regionalism, and is seen in Britain in the pressure for assemblies in Scotland and Wales, the recent establishment by the Yorkshire local authorities of a Yorkshire Assembly, and the appointment of a Minister for the South-West in response to regional pressure.

Once again, Europe is a factor in this equation. European regional funds go to regions, not countries. In areas such as the Highlands of Scotland most major infrastructure projects are being carried forward with European money. An office in Brussels is a priority for every regional and local development organisation, but not an office in London, because dealings with the British government are carried forward either through the Scottish, Welsh or Northern Ireland Offices, or through the government's Unified Regional Offices in the English regions.

So while as a matter of law Parliament's ultimate sovereignty remains intact, its influence has diminished over the years, and external developments, which it is unable to control, are tending to diminish that influence further.

Control of the Executive

The second of the three strands which I want to consider has a much longer pedigree than the first. Turning to Wade and Phillips again — but I could choose any constitutional textbook, of any period — I find this sentence:

The primary function of Parliament is the control of the executive.

Within Parliament itself, of course, that function is exercised principally by the House of Commons. The current edition of Erskine May,[1] the Parliamentary Bible, says this:

> The dominant influence enjoyed by the House of Commons within Parliament may be ascribed principally to its status as an elected assembly.... the House of Commons possesses the most important power vested in any branch of the legislature, the right of imposing taxes upon the people and of voting money for the public service. The exercise of this right ensures the annual meeting of Parliament for redress of grievances, and it may also be said to give the Commons the chief authority in the state.

But how true is that in practice? How far does the House of Commons control the executive? As long ago as 1955 in his 'Law and the Democratic State', Lord Radcliffe said this:

> The historic possibility of a clash between executive and Parliament has become an impossibility. There is nothing left but the political party in control of the House of Commons for the time being and having at its disposal by virtue of the control an unlimited executive power.

The dominance of the executive has undoubtedly rested on the party system, something which until recently was not formally recognised anywhere in our constitutional arrangements. Parties in themselves are in some ways a pragmatic response to the essential requirement of government — that it should have the means to govern, and a policy to follow.

The public consistently elects those who are put forward by the major parties and treats independent candidates harshly. On those occasions when an MP leaves his or her party, and stands as an independent or for another party, the times when the retained personal vote outweighs the party vote are so rare as to be almost insignificant. So is the true function of the legislature really to control the executive? Or does Parliament in fact have two roles — that of sustaining the executive, which it does well, and that of holding the executive to task, which it does less well?

The importance of the House of Commons as a proving ground for future ministers should not be underestimated. Of the 651 Members of Parliament over 100 are on the 'payroll' vote — that is, either government ministers or unpaid Parliamentary Private Secretaries — at any time, while nearly 100 more are opposition frontbenchers or members of their teams.

---

[1] Erskine May, *Parliamentary Practice*, 20th edn (1983).

So one-third of Members are either in executive office or on the career ladder towards it. The majority party also has the task of sustaining the government in office. Because Members depend on their party allegiance to secure election, the system of whipping is very strong indeed, and a Member who misses a three-line whip without permission will be left in no doubt that he or she has sinned. A Member whose unauthorised absence might affect the outcome of a vote will come under heavy pressure, while only a very limited number of abstentions from whipped votes on grounds of conscience will be tolerated. The role of sustaining the government does not sit well with the task of challenging it and holding it to task. Party political considerations inevitably enter into the process. Of course they should and must do so, and issues of policy are quite properly debated on a political basis. But instances do occur where the function of Parliament appears to suffer as a result. I have in mind the report by Sir Richard Scott on arms to Iraq.[2]

I am not going to try to judge the rights and wrongs of the arms to Iraq affair today. But I want to draw attention to the well documented tale in the Scott report of the continued reliance by government after government on 1939 emergency powers legislation as the basis for export control, for no better reason than that the Department of Trade was unwilling to expose its arrangements to proper Parliamentary scrutiny. It was made clear in 1939 that these powers were being sought for the duration of the wartime emergency alone. For that reason, the legislation, unusually, permitted subordinate legislation without any Parliamentary procedure. Sir Richard quoted 1984 advice to a DTI minister:

> It naturally remains possible that our continued reliance on this wartime legislation could become controversial at some time in the future.... However while the broad principles of new legislation which might be introduced now would not be particularly controversial, the detailed nature of the powers would not be agreed easily. Prolonged discussion might well be necessary with other Departments wanting more control over trade in certain products, and the [European] Commission (who might seek to curtail our freedom to control trade). *Parliament would no doubt insist on some degree of control (which at present does not exist).* [Emphasis added] We therefore recommend that the minister confirms his existing view that new legislation should be avoided.[3]

Now this may well not have been a very important piece of skulduggery by the executive. When it was eventually asked, 45 years after it should

---

[2] Report on the export of defence equipment to Iraq, HC 115 (1996).
[3] *Ibid.* p. 71, 17 August 1984.

have been, in the context of war with Iraq, the House had no hesitation in placing on a permanent footing executive powers, not subject to Parliamentary procedure, which had been granted originally to address a grave national emergency. But the ready acquiescence of Parliament in 1990, and its indifference in 1996 to the emergence of a sorry tale — perhaps because neither government nor opposition shows up well — indicate that the principles of its constitutional role have at times mattered less to the House of Commons than the practical politics of the day.

I have mentioned an area where the House has not appeared to do its job as well as we would like. In fairness, I should also draw attention to an area where great advances have been made in recent years. It was in 1979 that the House set up its present system of departmentally related Select Committees, with the task of scrutinising, investigating and influencing the work of individual government departments. These committees are now an established part of our constitution, supplementing the long-established scrutiny by the Public Accounts Committee. I am indebted to Peter Hennessy, who quotes in his book *The Hidden Wiring* some figures originally published by Philip Giddings in the journal *Parliamentary Affairs*:

> In [1992/93] the Departmental Select Committees held 663 meetings and issued 129 reports totalling 16,456 pages after 57 sessions with Cabinet ministers, 55 with ministers below Cabinet rank, 427 civil servants and 215 officials from so-called associated public bodies. To this one must add the Public Accounts Committee's 63 reports and 4,436 pages, the Select Committee on the Parliamentary Commissioner for Administration's 4 reports and 214 pages, and the Select Committee on European Legislation's 41 reports and 1,232 pages. In all 300 MPs were involved in this business.[4]

Through these committees the House now carries out a more direct and less politically charged scrutiny of the detailed work of the executive than ever before. Even if the public hears little of what goes on, there is no doubt that departments are significantly influenced by the committees. In my own committee's field, we were particularly struck by the work done by the Treasury and Civil Service Committee, which was almost entirely responsible for securing a new, and much needed, written civil service code.

Changes in the nature of the executive are, however, posing new challenges for Parliamentary and public scrutiny. My committee and I

---

[4] Peter Hennessy, *The Hidden Wiring* (1995), p. 154.

have already commented on these changes in reports and speeches. The executive is no longer monolithic and centralised. It comprises instead a great many different bodies, of varying size, structure and legal status. Many of them are local bodies, technically not even part of the public sector, but they all spend public money and provide public services. The scrutiny of these bodies, and the securing of effective accountability, is one of the great challenges which Parliament must face over the next few years. We have suggested that it cannot all be done at the centre and that accountability of local bodies, even if centrally funded, must be achieved at local level. It will be important for Parliament to ensure that the operational gains which have been achieved by the management revolution in the public services are not achieved at the expense of democratic control and accountability.

Public Standing and Perception

The third strand which I want to consider is the public standing and perception of Parliament, and particularly of the House of Commons. This is an issue which has been much in the news of late, and is closely related to the concerns about standards in public life which led to the establishment of the Nolan Committee. Standards in public life is, of course, yet another area in which Lord Radcliffe's name is to be found. He chaired both the inquiry following the Vassall scandal in the 1960s,[5] and the Committee on Ministerial Memoirs in the 1970s.[6] I do not want to rehearse in detail the analysis in our First Report, which examined and made recommendations about the standards of conduct of Members of Parliament. But there are some points which bear repeating.

Perhaps the most revealing was that we studied public opinion polls, which showed that only 14% of the British public trusted politicians to tell the truth. 64% of people thought that MPs made a lot of money from using public office improperly. That was 18% more people than ten years earlier. 87% thought MPs would tell lies if they thought the truth would hurt them politically. Yet we found that people generally took a different, and more positive view, of their own Member of Parliament. We also found that newspaper editors and journalists, who are in a position to know, did not believe that British politicians are generally corrupt, even though they promote public anxiety in order to sell their papers. Why is the public view so negative? To some extent it mirrors a general trend, which can be seen in other countries, of declining faith in political institutions. In a global

---

[5] Report of the Tribunal on the Vassall case, Cmnd 2009 (1963).
[6] Report of the Privy Counsellors on Ministerial Memoirs, Cmnd 6306 (1976).

village people are perhaps less inclined to believe that politicians have the capacity to match their promises with achievements, and so the political institutions themselves may be seen as less relevant.

But there is no doubt, either, that the House of Commons itself contributed to loss of public confidence by its failure to understand for itself that its rules and procedures for maintaining standards of conduct had not kept up with what is required of a modern institution. This can be understood most simply by considering politics as a profession. In recent years the disciplinary and complaints procedures of most self-respecting professions which serve the public have been overhauled to introduce equitable and open procedures, with independent elements. Parliament itself has imposed similar changes on elected politicians in local government. Yet until recently the House of Commons had no code of conduct for its Members, rules on what behaviour was and was not permissible which were unclear and contradictory, little routine enforcement of those rules, and inadequate procedures for investigating and adjudicating on complaints.

It is greatly to the credit of the House that once our report was published, and despite considerable initial misgivings, it grasped the nettle and introduced with commendable speed procedures which are closely based on our recommendations. There were those at the time who said that the appointment of the Parliamentary Commissioner for Standards would damage the reputation and authority of the House, because a public servant would be placed in a position of authority over elected Members of Parliament. The events of recent weeks, as the new system faces its first great test, demonstrate clearly that our proposals did not involve a further weakening of Parliament. What has been created is rather a much improved form of self-regulation, based on a code of conduct, clear rules, and sound arrangements for mounting an investigation and holding public hearings of evidence. I believe that, if at all possible, the behaviour of elected Members of Parliament, who do not actually break the law, should be judged by the House of Commons, and ultimately of course by the electorate, rather than by judges. No one who is familiar with our constitutional history would wish to see a return to the disputes between Parliament and the courts which characterised the seventeenth century in particular. The investigation which is now in progress, in what I might call the Hamilton case, is going to be the most difficult conceivable test for the new machinery, because the alleged actions under investigation occurred when the old, less satisfactory and, as I have said, inconsistent rules were in place. Should the House conclude the business thoroughly and impartially, without allowing political considerations to intrude, it will have taken a major step forward in rebuilding public confidence.

Conclusion

In one short lecture I do not pretend to have examined all aspects of the role of Parliament. I have not mentioned, for example, the future role of the House of Lords, or the potential impact of increasing its legitimacy by reducing the hereditary element on the balance of power between the two Houses. I have sought merely to set out a few of the major issues which cause difficulty for Parliament, and in particular for the House of Commons, as it contemplates its role in our constitution and system of government in the opening years of the next millennium.

Nor do I pretend to have solutions, or easy answers, to the problems which exist. Many Parliamentarians, commentators and academics are seeking to chart the way forward, and I can do no more than offer a few personal thoughts.

First, on the question of sovereignty and influence, my hope would be that Parliament will always look forwards, and seldom backwards. Everyone of my generation, who has lived through the repositioning of Britain in the world over the last half century, must feel a certain nostalgia for past greatness. There is nothing wrong with that, and we should be proud of our history and traditions. But the future must be determined by rational and hard-headed judgment of what is in our own best interests, which must include maintaining such fundamentally important principles as liberty, democracy, the rule of law and public morality. Those considerations apply as much to the role we retain for Westminster as to any other aspect of our national life. A serious debate about Europe is needed. What is not needed, and what demeans us as a nation, is our constant tendency to regard foreigners as inferior, to disparage their institutions, and to believe that oldest must necessarily be best. If the world around Parliament is changing, Parliament must look at how it can best contribute to and influence the good government of Britain in that changing world, and should not rule out the possibility of radical changes in its role and procedures.

That observation leads directly into the question of control of the executive. The time may well have come for Parliament to look again at the role of its committees, and in particular of its most powerful scrutiny body, the Public Accounts Committee. The PAC is the only committee which enjoys a strong supporting bureaucracy — the National Audit Office, headed by the Comptroller and Auditor General. But the PAC cannot possibly scrutinise directly all the thousands of autonomous, or quasi-autonomous, bodies which now provide public services. And the C & AG is prevented by statute from reviewing the merits of policies, so he cannot examine, to take an example which has been in the newspapers this week, whether or not the deregulation of buses has led to a more cost-effective and reliable bus service. Meanwhile the departmental select committees can and do look at policies, with the support of a handful of specialists and advisers. Parliament needs to consider whether the PAC should work more closely with the other committees, whether the inhibitions on the use of its own bureaucracy should be removed, and in particular whether new arrangements can be made, perhaps using regional select committees somewhat on the lines of the Scottish and Welsh Grand Committees, or by working with other bodies, such as local authorities, to scrutinise regional and local bodies more effectively.

The House of Commons has already shown its readiness to put in place the changes it has to restore public confidence in its standards of conduct. I think that more needs to be done to restore MPs' own confidence that they have a valuable and meaningful role to perform in contributing to the good government of Britain, and to demonstrate to potential Parliamentary candidates, and so to the public, that this is so. I am confident that the House itself recognises this. I hope that it will have the determination to act.

2. The Common Law and the Constitution

Sir Stephen Sedley

It is conventional wisdom, at least among lawyers, that the constitution of the United Kingdom is in its essentials the creation of the common law — an accretion of legal principles derived from judicial decisions which determine for the most part how the country is to be run from day to day. Apart from the historic texts — Magna Carta, the Bill of Rights — statutes were until this century regarded, by lawyers if not by Parliamentarians, as dangerous reefs in the great ocean of the common law, to be observed chiefly in order to circumnavigate them.[1] During this century the body of statute law has broken the surface at many points, forming sometimes small islands — such as the unnecessary but minor incursion of the legislature[2] into the judge-made law of judicial review — and sometimes great land-masses like the modern law of real property, supplanting the common law and equity, or whole continents of social and economic provision for which the common law itself has no remit.

Some of this legislation has been needed to get the common law out of holes into which it has dug itself. The common law's obsession with freedom of contract, to the exclusion of obvious disparities of bargaining power (though not of impediments to free trade), has repeatedly compelled Parliament to intervene in the interests of substantial justice.[3] Legislation

---

[1] E.g., Pollock, *Essays on Jurisprudence and Ethics* (1882), p. 85, cited by Lord Steyn in his 1996 Bentham Club presidential lecture: 'Parliament generally changes the law for the worse, and . . . the business of judges is to keep the mischief of its interference within the narrowest possible bounds'.

[2] Principally the Supreme Court Act 1981, s. 31(6).

[3] E.g., the Factories Acts and related industrial safety legislation, passed from 1833 onwards; the Rent Acts, initially passed during World War I to stop rackrenting of small tenements; the race, sex and disability discrimination laws; the hire purchase legislation; the Unfair Contract Terms Act 1977; and so forth. The principal point at which the common law has intervened is where unequal bargaining power has enabled one party to exact terms which stifle competition: here it will substitute its own view of what is reasonable as the criterion of legality.

has been needed, too, to bring into being systems of adjudication and distribution of public funds[4] in aid of schemes of social provision. Upon all of these, however, the common law in turn fixes its eye. It insists that, save where Parliament has plainly excluded it, every decision arrived at by the statutory tribunals which fix rents and decide on entitlements to benefit and so forth is to be reached only after a properly conducted hearing by a disinterested tribunal. And it has done the same, for reasons to which I shall return, in relation to bodies created not by Parliament but by ministers exercising the royal prerogative or by institutions setting out in the public interest to regulate themselves.

It is frequently said that in doing this — at least in relation to statutory bodies — the courts are simply giving effect to Parliament's unexpressed intention; or that Parliament today legislates in the knowledge, and therefore with the passive intent, that the common law will impose its own standards on the decision-makers on whom Parliament is conferring authority. Both views involve an imaginary individual whom one has to visualise as an officious backbencher (a cousin of the officious bystander who acts as referee when there is a debate about whether a term is to be implied in a contract). The officious backbencher rises to his feet in committee when a clause setting up some new decision-making process is being debated and says: 'Can the minister assure us that it is not intended that decisions should be taken under this measure without hearing both sides, or by someone with a stake in the outcome, or to the exclusion of relevant factors or in reliance on irrelevant ones, or in bad faith, or by someone who has taken leave of his senses?'; and the minister has to be visualised as replying, without even consulting his written briefing or turning in panic to a departmental official: 'Of course'.

The truth is both more difficult and more interesting. It was from the second quarter of the nineteenth century that Parliament, now increasingly representative and responsive, began to legislate in earnest — frequently on the basis of major Royal Commission reports — to regulate the chaos of early industrial and urban development. It imposed obligations on factory owners to take safety measures for their workers and on property owners to keep buildings in a safe state, and it set up powerful boards and commissions to oversee and regulate the profusion of railways, docks, canals and other enterprises which were threatening to destroy the conditions of their own existence. All of these were perceived by the propertied classes as dangerous invasions of individual liberty, and it was in order to restrain them that sympathetic mid-Victorian judges established many of the principles now familiar as the rules of modern public

---

[4] The national insurance and social security systems, to take only two examples.

law. In a pattern familiar in the United States today, they repeatedly granted orders of certiorari to bring up and quash regulatory decisions of these bodies, and when Parliament reacted by including no-certiorari clauses in its amending legislation, they granted prohibition and mandamus instead. It was by no means a one-way process. Although the judges made life difficult for some of the statutory canal and railway boards, they also used mandamus to compel reluctant local justices, most of whom were themselves employers, to convict mill owners of breaches of provisions of the Factories Acts designed to protect workers from injury or death. And when in 1863 a builder named Cooper found that the Wandsworth Board of Works had ordered him to pull down a house he owned without first giving him a chance to be heard, the Court of Exchequer struck down its order, not on the officious backbencher's ground that Parliament must have intended some form of hearing and had simply failed to say so, but on the judicial ground that where statute was silent the common law would speak in its own right. 'The justice of the common law,' said Byles J, 'will supply the omission of the legislature'.[5]

It is this alone which can furnish a consistent rationale for the now established power of judicial oversight of bodies which lack any statutory origin but which fulfil public functions: most notably the Criminal Injuries Compensation Board, which was set up in 1965 by means of a White Paper and was therefore the creation entirely of the executive, and the City Panel on Takeovers and Mergers, a voluntary body forming part of the City of London's procedures for self-regulation. Although it was only with the *GCHQ* case[6] in 1985 that the power of the courts to review exercises of the royal prerogative acquired its present profile, it was as early as 1967 that the power was established, when the Crown challenged the right of the High Court to entertain a dispute about whether the Criminal Injuries Compensation Board had acted in accordance with the remit contained in the White Paper which set it up.[7] It is not the leading judgment of Lord Parker CJ but the second one which today merits rereading, for there Diplock LJ observed that what was in dispute was the last unclaimed prize of the constitutional conflicts of the seventeenth century. Government had assumed that the exercise by ministers of the royal prerogative furnished the executive with a continuing residue of arbitrary power, questionable (if at all) in Parliament but beyond formal challenge in the courts. The assertion by the High Court that executive government possessed no such terrain of immunity was one of the great milestones on the road down which we are still moving towards government within the law. Twenty

[5] *Cooper* v *Wandsworth Board of Works* (1863) 14 CB NS 180.
[6] *Council of Civil Service Unions* v *Minister for the Civil Service* [1985] AC 374.
[7] *R* v *Criminal Injuries Compensation Board, ex parte Lain* [1967] 2 QB 864.

years later, in a case of comparable importance,[8] the Court of Appeal held that the court's writ ran to an entirely non-governmental body which nevertheless exercised power over matters of public concern. None of this jurisprudence is explicable as the simple implementation of Parliament's inarticulate wishes; it is, precisely, the justice of the common law which is in play.

In the light of this still contentious proposition, let me return to the metaphor of the constitution as a scattering of statutory islands in a sea of common law. The smallest and most picturesque of the islands are well enough known: Magna Carta, the Bill of Rights, the Act of Settlement, the Act of Union. But there are many others, larger and duller: the Representation of the People Acts, the Local Government Acts, the Tribunals and Inquiries Acts, the Judicature and Supreme Court Acts. These provide — to change the metaphor — the hardware of the machinery of state. The common law is one of the things — the software, if you like — that controls the operation of the machinery, but it is not the only thing. Within executive government a web of conventions is thought to provide procedures and assurances falling short of rules of law. And, far more potently, Parliament possesses its own law, its customs and privileges, which both respect and are respected by the common law.

What then is the modern role of the common law in the United Kingdom's constitution? Remember first that when you speak of the United Kingdom you are speaking of three separate jurisdictions. That of Northern Ireland has moved in fairly close conformity with that of England and Wales in terms of public law (though on some topics, notably the relationship of national security to public interest immunity, England and Wales could well learn from the jurisprudence of Northern Ireland),[9] but that of Scotland, although equally concerned with the invigilation of executive government and public administration, has been constrained both by its own tradition of law and by the continuing anomalies of Scotland's constitutional status to follow a perceptibly different course. What I have to say here relates principally to England and Wales, where modern judicial review has become surrounded by a mythology partly of its own making and partly generated by overheated media treatment. The vast majority of judicial review cases have little to do with the exercise of state power on any but the most routine level. They are last-ditch attempts to avoid deportation for breach of the immigration laws and rules or to secure housing as a homeless person. But there is no doubt that at the sharp

---

[8] *R v Panel on Takeovers and Mergers, ex parte Datafin Ltd* [1987] QB 815.

[9] See the judgment of Hutton CJ in *R v Belfast Coroner, ex parte MoD* (1994) NI CA transcript 2439–41, cited in *R v Home Secretary, ex parte McQuillan* [1995] 4 All ER 400, 418.

end of judicial review, the courts are from time to time called on to sit in judgment on ministers and their departments on issues which would until recently have been regarded as matters of policy, and to do so on the application of people who might until recently have been regarded as having no right to be heard.

It is this incremental readiness to take a hard look at the legality of acts of government, and not (as law students continue to be taught) a sudden postwar flash of light in the *Wednesbury* case, which represents the modern sea change in public law. It was in fact the Victorian judges, as I have illustrated, who were responsible for first turning judicial review into a developed system for supervising the lower courts and official bodies to whom state power was being systematically delegated. It is in their judgments that you will first find the tests of lawful decision-making which Lord Greene MR later summarised in the *Wednesbury* case, a decision which introduces no new doctrine of law and of which the outcome exemplifies the state of torpor into which English public law had descended by 1948.[10] The reasons for the decline are still little explored. It can be seen setting in at the time of the Great War,[11] partly no doubt because of a sense that to challenge government in a time of crisis would be unpatriotic, but partly too, I believe, because there was now in place the career civil service which Northcote, Trevelyan and others had agitated for in the 1860s, and which by the turn of the century was filling the top echelons of Whitehall with the best brains from the best schools and universities — men in whose capacity for sound public administration not only ministers but judges could feel entire confidence. The departments of state which they ran in turn took responsibility for the plethora of adjudicative tribunals and boards which administered the state at local level, again making judicial invigilation of these appear unnecessary. The fact that the one element of the state over which central government had no immediate control, elected local authorities, continued to attract the sharp eye of the law, provoking the celebrated denunciation by the House of Lords of the surcharged Poplar councillors,[12] supports this thesis. The inter-war years correspondingly, as is generally now agreed, saw executive government achieve a consolidation of state power unequalled before

---

[10] [1948] 1 KB 223. The Court of Appeal upheld the Divisional Court in refusing to interfere with what the courts might regard today as an abuse of power by a local authority, which had used its cinema licensing functions in order to stop children going to the pictures on Sundays. The real issue was collateral purpose — but this was neither argued in terms nor addressed in Lord Greene MR's now famous exegesis.

[11] *Local Government Board* v *Arlidge* [1915] AC 120.

[12] *Roberts* v *Hopwood* [1925] AC 578 (denouncing the councillors' 'eccentric principles of socialist philanthropy' and their 'feminist ambition to secure the equality of the sexes in the matter of wages').

or since. In a period of changing governments and political and economic instability Parliament itself may well have welcomed this anchorage, as ministers and policies came and went. The fact that in the same period — indeed in the same year, 1929 — Lord Hewart CJ (who had previously been a member of the government as Attorney-General) published his book *The New Despotism* fulminating at the impotence of the courts in the face of statutes giving the executive powers of primary legislation, while the Permanent Secretary to the Lord Chancellor, Sir Claud Schuster, asserted in a private memorandum that in recent years 'the weight of prejudice against the State in the minds of many members of the Court of Appeal and Judges of the High Court has been such as seriously to affect the Administration of Justice',[13] may well demonstrate how different contemporary perceptions are from the judgment of history (and may also call in question the picture given by the law reports of the period) but does not fundamentally challenge the pattern of executive supremacism and judicial passivity between the wars.

It was into this culture of judicial passivity — the object of Lord Atkin's now celebrated protest[14] — and of corresponding administrative self-assurance that the 1945 Labour government came with a solid majority and a mandate for radical change. There is little doubt that it is to that culture that it owed both its political achievements and its relative freedom from successful legal challenge.[15] The legal literalism of Lord Simonds LC, which has become a byword for narrow formalism, was no more than part of an entire mood of legal minimalism which left the Chancery Division with a shortage of work and put the Bar into a numerical decline that was not reversed until the late 1960s. There is also evidence of conscious judicial abstention from anything that might be seen as political interference.[16] It is in the decades since then that a major shift has occurred

---

[13] Quoted in Robert Stevens, *The Independence of the Judiciary* (1993), p. 27.

[14] *Liversidge* v *Anderson* [1942] AC 206, 244–5

[15] Most notably in the protection afforded by the House of Lords in *Franklin* v *Minister of Town and Country Planning* [1948] AC 87 to what would today seem a clear case of prejudgment.

[16] See Sir Leslie Zines, *Constitutional Change in the Commonwealth* (1991), pp. 36–7, describing how in the early 1950s Sir Raymond Evershed MR told Australian lawyers that 'it was believed by many when the Attlee government was elected in 1945 that, based on past performance, the courts of England would emasculate any social welfare or other collectivist legislation by that government.... [H]e was pleased to say that that had not happened. The judges had not sabotaged the social welfare state.' The reference to 'past performance' is interesting: it may relate to the Privy Council's wrecking of Canada's New Deal legislation in 1937 (*A-G for Canada* v *A-G for Ontario* [1937] AC 326; *A-G for British Columbia* v *A-G for Canada* [1937] AC 105) or perhaps to the years before the Great War when Farwell LJ in *Dyson*'s case [1911] KB 410 felt able to characterise the courts as 'the only defence of the liberty of the subject against departmental aggression'.

in the structures which hold Parliament, judiciary and executive in an ordered relationship with one another. Such shifts are in principle not only predictable but necessary: like the joists and beams of a house, they will not be efficient unless there is room for a certain amount of movement. Lord Diplock, looking back from the vantage point of 1982,[17] described it as a purely reactive process by which the judges had moved to 'preserve the integrity of the rule of law' in the face of 'changes in the social structure, methods of government and the extent to which the activities of private citizens are controlled by governmental authorities, that have been taking place, sometimes slowly, sometimes swiftly, since the rules were originally propounded. Those changes' — he added significantly — 'have been particularly rapid since World War II'. Coming as they did from the judge who perhaps more than any other deserves recognition as the engineer, if not the architect, of modern public law, whose sense of history and policy was acute, and to whom the throwaway remark was a foreign concept, these reflections are important. Lord Diplock acknowledges and asserts the function of public law as a source of enforceable standards in public administration; but he describes these as changing manifestations of a constant principle, the rule of law, and not as a series of shifts in the law designed to meet shifts in the polity.

For my part I would think this distinction, though relevant, is more presentational than analytical. The reality is that standards of justice do change. One member of the court which decided *Cooper* v *Wandsworth Board of Works* was the judge who had tried the case at first instance — something regarded as normal then and as wholly unacceptable now. I would prefer to live with the fact that even something as basic as the norms of due process can change, rather than try to argue that justice is a metaphysical constant of which only the manifestations change in response to changes in the wider world. But the importance of Lord Diplock's account is that it acknowledges the interventionist role of modern public law, in particular in maintaining legal standards within changing modes of government. This may, first of all, afford some explanation of the early reawakening of modern public law in the *Northumberland* case in 1952[18] as a reaction against the corporatism which the consensus politics of the wartime and post-war years were threatening to turn into a permanent feature of the state; for it was from this point that the Divisional Court and the Court of Appeal, displaying an impressive grasp of legal history, swept judicial and administrative acts back into a unitary system of supervisory control. Secondly, it offers a

---

[17] *R* v *Inland Revenue Commissioners, ex parte National Federation of the Self-Employed* [1982] AC 617, 639–40.

[18] *R* v *Northumberland Compensation Appeal Tribunal, ex parte Shaw* [1952] 1 KB 338.

coherent explanation of the subsequent growth of public law doctrines —
which, however, has not itself been entirely coherent, and to which I shall
return. Thirdly, and within this process of growth, it may help to explain
the continuing momentum of public law during and since the 1980s. This
period has witnessed a shift within government from an inherited culture
of cautious and deliberative policy formation and implementation, always
trammelled and sometimes paralysed by legal advice, to a more muscular
culture of determined decision-making. The shift itself is a fact of political
history with which the courts have no immediate concern. But in the light
of it it is unsurprising that the traditional process of prior caution which
one distinguished former Treasury counsel has described[19] has yielded to
a process in which legal challenge, instead of being an occasional and
unexpected obstacle, becomes an occupational hazard of the conduct of
government.

The problem of lawfulness of government action, in other words, has
never been absent: what has shifted is the forum in which it is typically
resolved. The *Pergau Dam* case[20] is a good example: it is now known that
ministers did not consult the Foreign and Commonwealth Office's own
lawyers before deciding to make the subvention which, on subsequent
challenge, was held by the court to be unlawful. In an earlier period it is
almost certain that the issue, although it would have arisen, would not have
reached the courts: it would have been considered departmentally and if
necessary with the advice of Treasury counsel, and if its legality had been
thought doubtful it would have been modified or dropped. There is nothing
necessarily wrong with a policy of doing what is thought best and leaving
any legal challenges to the courts; but it is hardly reasonable to criticise
the courts if they then entertain some of the challenges which are brought
and occasionally uphold them. (You can sometimes find the same
newspaper criticising judicial intervention in state policy in a judgment of
which it disapproves and on the next page cheering a victory for somebody
whose rights the court has vindicated against the state.) The same may
well be true of the public controversy between senior judges and ministers
about changes to the criminal justice system: not many years ago the issues
which have now become public property would have been resolved by a
quiet word and a rethink; but here, where not legality but policy is at issue,

---

[19] The Rt Hon Sir Harry Woolf (Second Street Lecture) [1986] PL 220, 221–2: he speaks
of '. . . a change in the standards of public bodies large and small. It used to be the case
that, if the legality of a course of action was in doubt, it was not adopted. Now it appears
to be [be]coming a case of anything is permissible unless and until it is stopped by the
courts'.

[20] *R v Secretary of State for Foreign and Commonwealth Affairs, ex parte World
Development Movement Ltd* [1995] 1 WLR 386.

there is force in the view that the change, though embarrassing, is for the better, bringing the issue out of the inaccessible corridors of power and into the open space of public debate where it properly belongs.

The other chief reason why the *Pergau Dam* subvention was able to be adjudicated on is that the courts have in recent years opened their doors wider to applicants who have nothing personally or collectively to gain from the resolution of the issue but who have a respectable reason for bringing it before the court. This again is not new. In 1916, when anti-German feeling was at its height, an individual named Sir George Makgill obtained leave to seek orders barring two citizens of German extraction, Sir Edgar Speyer and Sir Ernest Cassel, from remaining in office as Privy Counsellors. What is interesting about the case is not that he lost but that both the Divisional Court, presided over by Lord Reading CJ, and the Court of Appeal entertained it when Makgill manifestly had no personal stake in the outcome. Lord Reading said:

> Sir George Makgill appears to have brought this matter before the court on purely public grounds without any private interest to serve, and it is to the public advantage that the law should be declared by judicial authority. I think the court ought to incline to the assistance, and not to the hindrance, of the applicant.[21]

He drew authority, in turn, from a decision of an eighteenth-century Chief Justice, Lord Kenyon, who — now two centuries ago — said:

> I do not mean to say that a stranger may not in any case prefer this sort of application, but he ought to come to the court with a very fair case in his hands.[22]

It is the reopening of standing which, although not responsible for more than a handful of cases, signals the contemporary shift of public law from a system which merely offers a different pathway to the vindication of private rights to a principled system of invigilation of the legality of governmental action. It focuses attention, in particular, on the fact that public law is concerned not necessarily with rights (which inhere in individuals) but with wrongs in the conduct of the state (which may but do not necessarily invade individual rights).

But the shift is by no means entirely the doing of the courts. Not only have the courts been obliged to take on the invigilation of the two major statutory systems I have already mentioned — immigration and asylum,

---

[21] *R v Speyer* [1916] 1 KB 595, DC; upheld [1916] 2 KB 858, CA
[22] *R v Kemp* (1789) 1 East 46, n.

housing and housing benefits — in order to ensure both that Parliament's laws are properly applied and that the procedures by which they are applied are themselves fair and above board; they have been given by Parliament the obligation, under the European Communities Act 1972, of ensuring that both ministerial measures having the force of law and Parliament's own statutes conform to the law of what is now the European Union. The European Court of Justice has made it plain that where domestic law conflicts with European law the court's duty is to limit or strike down the former.[23] To characterise this process as judicial suprem-acism, when it is Parliament which has consciously legislated to produce it, requires a fair measure of intellectual perversity — yet it forms part of a press arsenal directed in recent years at the judiciary, about which I shall have something shortly to say.

Before I do so, however, there is a further dimension of the European Communities Act which is worth noting. Its effect has been to reverse the presumption that a later statute overrides an earlier inconsistent one, not generally but in the special case where a later domestic statute clashes with a European law given effect by the European Communities Act 1972, as the Merchant Shipping Act 1988 did. This may sound minor, but it represents a substantial qualification of a tenet of our constitution — that no Parliament may bind its successors. It is the courts, moreover, which have necessarily had the task of establishing this qualification, and in doing so they have given us, in effect, a fundamental law — one with which other legislation must conform. Such a law is, precisely, a constitutional instrument. It is, however, not entrenched in the way the United States constitution is: it can be repealed or amended by a simple majority and without any special procedure. Seen in this light, it is not unique. There is much to be said for the view that the Bill of Rights 1689 is an original instrument of the same kind: it was adopted during a brief period when Britain had neither a king nor a parliament (James II having first dissolved Parliament and then died) by an ad hoc convention which offered William of Orange the Crown, accompanied by a Declaration of Rights which the convention, endorsed the next year by a lawfully summoned parliament, passed into law as the Bill of Rights. The Bill of Rights can therefore be said, historically at least, to be the terms upon which the Crown itself holds power. Yet the Royal Assent has only this year been given to an amendment of Article 9 of it, permitting MPs to waive a constitutional immunity from the questioning in other forums of what they say in Parliament — an immunity which was widely thought to be Parliament's own and not a personal protection for individual MPs —

---

[23] *Factortame (No. 2)* [1991] 1 AC 603.

in order to allow them to bring libel actions with greater freedom.[24] Our fundamental laws, in other words, are at bottom statutes like any other. But the fundamentality of the European Communities Act, so long as it is on the statute book, is undoubtedly of a new kind, giving the courts the power and the obligation to cut down domestic statutes which offend against European law and representing, therefore, a major hiatus created by Parliament in its own sovereignty.

Why then is it that these two things — the conscientious enforcement of Parliament's statutes and the continued adaptation of the common law to the needs of a changing world — have been presented to the newspaper-reading public as a conflict between ministers and judges, the broadsheets on the whole supporting continued judicial invigilation of executive government, the tabloids for the most part suggesting a comprehensive judicial assault on the foundations of democracy? To answer the question, it is first relevant to point out the frailty of the premise on which the tabloid attacks have been based. The premise is that executive government, since it derives its authority from a majority in the House of Commons and is in turn answerable through ministers to Parliament, speaks for the people, so that those who challenge government are challenging democracy. For a series of reasons both of practice and of principle, this is entirely misleading. A democracy is more than a state in which power resides in the hands of a majority of elected representatives: it is a state in which individuals and minorities have an assurance of certain basic protections from the majoritarian interest, and in which independent courts of law hold the responsibility for interpreting, applying and — importantly — supplementing the law laid down by Parliament in the interests of every individual, not merely of the represented majority. It is also, in modern conditions, a state in which public administration at many levels requires on the one hand considerable freedom to form and implement policy and on the other constant invigilation both by Parliament, to ensure that executive policy and practice conform to its wishes, and by the courts, to ensure that they conform to the law. Because Parliament lacks the resources to govern directly (a consequence in part of the sheer complexity of modern government, but in part of Parliament's own inefficient use of its powers and underfunding of its personnel), enormous tranches of public power have been and continue to be delegated to ministers by statutes which enable them — indeed, require them — to legislate by proxy. Parliamentary scrutiny of these measures,

---

[24] Defamation Act 1996, s. 13, giving 'a person' the right to waive 'the protection of any enactment or rule of law which prevents proceedings in Parliament being impeached or questioned in any court or place out of Parliament' — i.e., Article 9 of the Bill of Rights. It is not entirely clear whether a person other than an MP can use this right.

even in the minority of cases where they require the affirmative approval of both Houses, is rarely close and often cursory.

But it is precisely because ministerial government in consequence enjoys a high degree of autonomy, enabling it in large part to control the Parliament to which it is theoretically subordinate, that it is crucial to stress the constitutional fact that the executive does not possess anything which can accurately be called sovereignty. It is in Parliament and the courts, each exercising a discrete though interdependent function of the state, the legislative and the judicial, that the sovereignties of the state reside.[25] The executive has a huge range of functions which are exclusive to it, but neither politically nor legally does it have the last word: as its name suggests, it carries out what the legislature or the royal prerogative confides to it in whatever ways the law permits.

It is a necessary condition of this dual sovereignty that each body should respect the territory of the other, and since the seventeenth century Parliament and the courts have been remarkably successful in this. At the start of the eighteenth century, when Holt CJ was hearing argument in the great constitutional case of *Ashby* v *White*,[26] the Speaker of the House appeared with his retinue and threatened to have Holt impeached for contempt of Parliament; but he desisted when Holt threatened to have him imprisoned for contempt of court, and the consequent stand-off between legislature and judiciary has held ever since. What matters greatly, however, is where ministers as the heads of the executive departments of state have stood since then. They have stood answerable to Parliament (if they were members of either House) on matters of policy and to the courts on matters of law. When a Home Secretary, Lord Halifax, was sued for punitive damages for having unlawfully authorised the raid on the *North Briton*,[27] Lord Wilmot CJ told the jury: 'The law makes no difference between great and petty officers. Thank God, they are all amenable to justice....' — and the jury found accordingly. And when a later Home Secretary, Kenneth Baker, ignored a court order requiring him to bring back a Zairean asylum seeker whom his department had deported while he

---

[25] See Lord Bridge of Harwich in *X Ltd* v *Morgan-Grampian (Publishers) Ltd* [1991] 1 AC 1, 48: 'The maintenance of the rule of law is in every way as important in a free society as the democratic franchise. In our society the rule of law rests upon twin foundations: the sovereignty of the Queen in Parliament in making the law and the sovereignty of the Queen's courts in interpreting and applying the law'.

[26] (1703) 2 Ld Raym 938; Holt KB 524. The confrontation with the Speaker is recorded in the DNB entry on Holt. Less than a decade earlier the Speaker had also been the Master of the Rolls — Sir John Trevor, who in 1695 was impeached and fined (after a debate over which he himself initially presided) for accepting a large fee from the Common Council of London to bring forward a Bill in the House.

[27] *Wilkes* v *Lord Halifax* (1769) 19 St Tr 1406.

was seeking the protection of the courts, the House of Lords in a major vindication of the rule of law held him guilty, in his official capacity, of contempt of court.[28] Few things could illustrate more sharply the distinct and parallel sovereignties of Parliament and the courts on the one hand, and the limits of ministerial autonomy on the other. Indeed, the relative immunity of ministers from Parliamentary sanctions, now that ministers no longer fall on their swords when a departmental disaster occurs, has thrust into greater prominence the role of the courts as guardians of the standards of lawful ministerial action. It also illustrates the fragility of convention as a source of constitutional law.

Giving judgment in the Zairean refugee's case, Lord Nolan, then a member of the Court of Appeal, adopted a formulation which I had tentatively advanced as counsel in the case: 'The proper constitutional relationship of the executive with the courts is that the courts will respect all acts of the executive within its lawful province, and that the executive will respect all decisions of the courts as to what its lawful province is'.[29] If, as I continue to believe, this is a correct appreciation not only of the governing principle but of what the relationship is in practice, the suggestion that judicial review of the executive represents a usurpation of democracy is the reverse of the truth. It is also unsustainable on a more detailed inspection. Ministers are no more elected than judges are: both are appointed to office by the Sovereign on the advice of the government of the day. It is judicial independence, an essential component of any democracy, which dictates that judges are not answerable to Parliament, just as Parliamentary sovereignty dictates Parliament's immunity from judicial adjudication. But while ministers are accountable legally to the courts and politically to Parliament, there is no constitutional requirement that ministers must be accountable to the representatives of the electorate. Those who are peers answer only to the unelected chamber. Moreover neither law nor convention requires them to be members of either House: in recent decades at least two persons[30] have held ministerial office when they were neither MP nor peer.

Others must say why, in spite of these elementary constitutional facts, much of the press has in recent times insistently suggested that executive government is the pinnacle of the democratic structure and that judges who overset ministerial decisions are overstepping their powers and jeopardising democracy. I merely note that the main spate of such criticism coincided with the gestation of two major reports which government was awaiting with natural concern: Lord Nolan's first report

---

[28] *M v Home Office* [1994] AC 377.

[29] [1992] QB 270, 314.

[30] Patrick Gordon Walker and Frank Cousins.

on standards in public life and Sir Richard Scott's report on the arms for Iraq affair. For comprehensible reasons these two distinguished figures were not the sole or even the principal focus of the critiques: the campaign instead sought out other judges whose work impinged on matters of policy, repeatedly suggesting that as a group the judiciary were determined to interfere with things which neither experience nor status qualified them to deal with. With the publication of the two reports the campaign has perceptibly died down. It prompts one further reflection. The lobby system, by which journalists are fed government's own version of events, depends for its existence on the lack of open access to government information. If on these issues — which by definition are not confidential — the public had ready access to government data, there would be no reason (other than the unthinkable ones of venality or idleness) for journalists to look to government spokesmen for their copy, and there would equally be a more closely defined basis upon which government could filter information for public consumption. The experience of Sir Richard Scott in finding that every step he took in an endeavour to be as open as possible in completing and presenting his report became the source of pre-emptive counter-strikes designed to undermine it illustrates how far we have travelled away from received notions of public probity.

Does — or should — the common law have anything to say about the conduct of holders of public office, either ministerial or official, in this no man's land on the peripheries of Whitehall, where the court's writ runs, and of Westminster, where it does not? If, for example, the High Court's attention had been drawn to the fact that a Member of Parliament was prepared to put questions to ministers in return for money payments, could it and should it have been prepared to grant an injunction or an order of prohibition against the MP? Probably not, since what the Member does on the floor and within the precincts of the House in his or her capacity as an MP is a matter for Parliament alone, even if it might be questioned whether the making of an arrangement to receive a lobbyist's money in return for doing something an MP would not otherwise be doing is an act lying within the role or functions of an MP. But would this mean that the lobbyist necessarily enjoyed a similar constitutional protection from the attentions of the common law? To take a different example, at least one MP in the past held the view that the Parliamentary Ombudsman is an unconstitutional office and was unwilling to refer legitimate constituents' complaints to the Ombudsman. Could and should the courts have been prepared to require him to do so? There is nothing, it seems, that Parliament itself can do about it; yet it is Parliament which has legislated to give access to the Ombudsman through MPs. Would the court's ordinary obligation to give effect to such legislation meet an immovable object in the privileges of

Parliament, or would the courts be expected by Parliament itself to prevent the obstruction of an important channel of recourse for citizens against the state?

Let me turn to another group of constitutional problems. Probably the most valuable guide to a Bill going through Parliament are the Notes on Clauses prepared by the drafter[31] to explain the intended effect of the measure. White Papers no doubt help, but they have a public relations function which can diminish their utility. Ministers have the Notes on Clauses to hand; the public do not; nor does the opposition except in those cases (now a growing number) where a copy is made available to them — although, for reasons which I have not heard respectably explained, this may be a different version from that provided to ministers. It is principally from these notes, supplemented by departmental briefings, that ministers answer questions about legislative intent, and since the decision of the House of Lords in *Pepper* v *Hart*[32] it is from ministerial answers that in cases of ambiguity or obscurity the courts will derive the true meaning of the eventual legislation. Ought not the courts, as well as any seriously interested member of the public, to be entitled to a sight of the Notes on Clauses — not when they are lodged 30 years later in the Public Record Office but when they matter? If so, is their disclosure a matter of Parliamentary grace — in which case it is beyond the purview of the courts — or of ministerial discretion? If the latter, is it a discretion which, like other discretions, has legal limits; and if so, what are they? There may be no private law right to such access, but public law, as I have said, is concerned centrally with wrongs rather than rights. May it be a misuse of public power to deny the public access to non-confidential departmental information without good reason?

I pose these not as rhetorical questions but as topics for study and debate. Court-watchers need not imagine that they represent some judicial agenda. Whether because of press agitation or because of the natural trajectory of the pendulum of legal policy, or — as I think likeliest — because of the enduring quandary of the common law in its endeavour to be simultaneously certain and adaptable, there is unlikely to be any major change in public law's hesitantly incremental process of growth. If there was a point of overreaching, it was probably in the early 1980s when not central but local government was so cowed by the adverse decision of the House of Lords in the *Fares Fair* case[33] that the GLC found itself taking

---

[31] In preference to 'draftsman' I have used the inclusive word adopted by Francis Bennion, himself a distinguished past holder of the office, in his *Statutory Construction*.

[32] [1993] AC 593. In my next lecture I consider some of the constitutional implications of this case.

[33] *Bromley LBC* v *GLC* [1983] 1 AC 768. For an authoritative evaluation of the decision see M. Loughlin, *Legality and Locality* (OUP, 1996), pp. 231–47.

counsel's opinion on whether it could renovate the lifts at Goodge Street station. If thereafter things have quietened down, it is because subsequent delegated legislation to cap the raising of local revenues has been upheld by the courts of judicial review, leaving local government to adjust to its new role of local administration of central government policy. In jurisdictional terms, the growth of public law in these years, beyond the control of the use of royal prerogative, has been modest. The further expansionism of *Datafin* (itself modest enough in practice)[34] has been offset by the retreat in the *Aga Khan*[35] case from what many would regard as the same principle of judicial control of monopolies of power. The emergence of a duty to give reasons, regarded by many people today as fundamental to all good public administration, has got stuck at a point where Home Office ministers do[36] but university teachers do not have to give reasons for decisions of comparable importance to the individuals concerned.[37] The retreat in the *Rose Theatre* case[38] and the subsequent advance in the *Greenpeace* case[39] have only brought us back to where we were in 1916 on the topic of *locus standi*. We have extended the substantive grounds of review to meet the demands of fairness in modern public administration by developing the still incomplete doctrine of legitimate expectation; but in spite of Lord Diplock's anticipatory welcome more than a decade ago,[40] we have not embraced the doctrine of proportionality which our Continental partners seem at home with. The continuing growth in the length of the Crown Office list does not significantly reflect such broadening of jurisdiction as there has been. It reflects far more a growing (though geographically extremely uneven)[41]

---

[34] [1987] QB 815. The Court of Appeal made it clear that, having asserted its jurisdiction, it would not expect to exercise it by means of coercive orders.

[35] *R v Jockey Club, ex parte Aga Khan* [1993] 1 WLR 909.

[36] *R v Home Secretary, ex parte Doody* [1994] 1 AC 531.

[37] *R v Higher Education Funding Council, ex parte Institute of Dental Surgery* [1994] 1 WLR 242. I acknowledge the force of Professor Paul Craig's critique in his article 'The common law, reasons and administrative justice' [1994] CLJ 282, 299–300. He argues that my judgment in that case has failed to square the circle. The circle is the current doctrine that reasons must be given in a still undefined class of cases, but that there is no general duty to give reasons: *R v Home Secretary, ex parte Doody* (note 36 above). To square it the courts would have at least to go on to hold that there is a general public law duty to give reasons, but that it is subject to exceptions — which would then have to be identified case by case. It is doubtful, however, whether an attempt to resolve it by legislation would fare any better.

[38] *R v Secretary of State for the Environment, ex parte Rose Theatre Trust* [1990] 1 QB 504.

[39] *R v HM Inspectorate of Pollution, ex parte Greenpeace Ltd (No. 2)* [1994] 4 All ER 329.

[40] *Council of Civil Service Unions v Minister for the Civil Service* [1985] AC 374.

[41] Sunkin, Bridges, Meszaros, *Judicial Review in Perspective*, 2nd ed. (Public Law Project, 1995).

awareness among lawyers and to a lesser extent the public that in certain fields it is possible to challenge public administrators in court. It also, inevitably, brings a drop in the quality of presentation and argument: advocates now use the word '*Wednesbury*' as an expletive ('My Lord, this was *Wednesbury* unfair'); they toss in irrationality or legitimate expectation in the hope that these will stick to something in the papers; or sometimes they simply busk it, advancing grounds like one that recently came before me: 'The respondent has reached a decision which no other Secretary of State could have reached'. But it is on the whole only the Crown Office list judges who suffer by this slide of more into worse; I believe the leave process, onerous as it is, works tolerably well in filtering out the non-starters. What has changed, without doubt, is the readiness of the courts to take tenable challenges seriously and to exact high standards of fairness and legality in public administration. If we no longer decide cases in the administration-minded way in which leading cases earlier this century[42] seem to modern eyes to have been decided, it is, I suggest, because the common law has tried conscientiously to maintain the rule of law in a polity characterised as never before by continents of statute law, rafts of delegated ministerial powers and muscular policy imperatives. If so, it has been performing its proper role within our organic constitution.[43]

---

[42] I have instanced, in this paper, the *Wednesbury* and *Franklin* cases. Although current demonology singles out the 1915 case of *Arlidge* as the start of the decline, *Arlidge* could well go the same way today given its legislative context.

[43] Among many valuable contributions to this standpoint, I would single out T.R.S. Allan, 'Legislative supremacy and the rule of law' [1985] CLJ 111, 112: 'The existing potential for natural constitutional development through judicial decision should at least be recognised. It is only in that context that we can decide whether or not the risks of radical reform are worth embracing, or whether we may inadvertently destroy what is of fundamental value in our polity.'

3. The Executive

Rt Hon Lord Nolan

INTRODUCTION

When Lord Radcliffe examined relations between the state and the individual in the Reith lectures of 1951, he entitled the series 'The Problem of Power'. In his concluding talk he observed:

> It has been part of the cant of English life for so long to speak of power as an evil thing, an intoxicating thing, a corrupting thing.[1]

Asquith, when prime minister, claimed that he had no power — 'Power, power,' he said, 'you may think you are going to get it, but you never do'. He convinced no one. The British have always been suspicious of power, and of those who exercise it. In recent years suspicion has deepened into a profound scepticism about the motives and intentions of those in public life. A 1993 poll revealed that a mere 11% of the population would trust a government minister to tell the truth. 'Politicians generally' scored only 14%.

It is not difficult to suggest reasons for this. Politicians constantly accuse each other, sometimes persuasively, of dishonesty. The speed and intrusiveness of press and television reporting, coupled with a tendency to sacrifice accuracy and detail for colour and immediacy, often result in the truth being obscured or distorted. The lack of excitement and appeal of the political process in an age when all the great ideological debates seem to have been settled and major parties in all countries seem to talk the same language, breeds cynicism.

It is also relevant that, in this country, many of the limits placed on the exercise of government power have traditionally been conventional, rather than legal. To command confidence they have rested on a belief in the British capability for good government — what has been called by Professor Peter Hennessey the 'good chaps' theory of government.[2] In

---

[1] Lord Radcliffe, *The Problem of Power*, Reith Memorial Lectures 1951 (London, 1952).
[2] Peter Hennessy, *The Hidden Wiring* (London, 1975).

recent years, of course, the extension in the scope of judicial review has subjected the exercise of authority to new disciplines. But much still rests on vague and unspoken conventions that such and such is the 'right' way to do things. One of the most important areas covered by these conventions is accountability.

Ministers and Civil Servants

In this second lecture I want to examine the accountability of the executive, but I must first define what I mean by the executive. It is possible to define the executive widely, to include all those bodies responsible for the development of policies and the provision of services throughout the public sector. However, the great majority of those bodies are creatures of statute, set up under Act of Parliament, regulated under provisions contained in Acts of Parliament, and with no powers other than those expressly entrusted to them by Parliament. Into this category come familiar institutions which many people may well have come to regard as part of the constitution, such as local authorities, the police and the armed forces, as well as newer and less familiar bodies such as English Heritage, the Welsh Development Agency and Scottish Homes, which are often seen simply as arms of government.

The narrower definition, which I shall adopt tonight, holds that the executive is simply the Crown, represented for practical purposes by ministers of the Crown, and their servants, the civil service. There are some important constitutional elements which distinguish the executive narrowly defined in this way from the wider spread of statutory bodies. Traditionally, the Crown had always governed by virtue of the royal prerogative, which has been constrained by the Crown's acceptance — voluntarily or otherwise — of restrictive Acts of Parliament. The seminal Act of this kind was, of course, the Bill of Rights. Over the centuries, the extent to which the actions of the executive have been regulated by and subject to statute has grown steadily, but there remains a strong residual prerogative power, exercised theoretically by the Crown but in practice by ministers. A simple example of the special position of the Crown was seen three years ago when the Queen voluntarily agreed to pay income tax. This change was a reminder that the tax statutes do not apply to the Crown. Until recently Crown exemption from the impact of Acts of Parliament has been far from exceptional: it has been the norm. Government departments for many years complied with health and safety legislation, planning legislation and many similar laws on a voluntary basis, because the statutes did not bind the Crown. It was long thought unwise to collide with a Post Office van because, as Crown vehicles, they were exempt from the statutory requirement to hold motor insurance, and any claim had to be pursued with the GPO itself.

It is only recently that the trend has been for new legislation to bind the Crown. One factor has been Parliament's relatively new select committees, which I mentioned in my first lecture. They have exerted pressure on departments to restrict use of prerogative powers to emergency situations only, and to regularise any such actions rapidly through legislation. The use of the prerogative has thus greatly diminished in recent years, but it is by no means dead. And one of the main areas where it is exercised is in the organisation and structure of the executive.

Ministers, then, are ministers of the Crown. In theory they hold office on the sufferance of the monarch and are accountable to her. Once upon a time, that was the true state of affairs. The monarch would choose ministers to form a government, and dismiss them at will. With the withdrawal of the monarch from direct political involvement, the British executive and legislature became collocated, and by the nineteenth century the convention of ministerial accountability to Parliament had become fully established.

Civil servants, too, are servants of the Crown, and their origins were similar to those of ministers. Hence the formal titles of senior officials and junior ministers are distinguishable, even today, only by the civil service prefix of 'permanent': as in 'permanent under-secretary of state' for the civil service head of a department.

In the nineteenth century, however, the politicians and the officials were separated. The famous report of Sir Stafford Northcote and Sir Charles Trevelyan,[3] implemented for the home civil service by Gladstone in his first ministry, replaced a system of patronage which would undoubtedly have led in the modern era to the 'spoils' system as practised in the United States and elsewhere.

Northcote–Trevelyan's proposals must be counted a tremendous success. Although their concern was purely with systems of appointment, the logical consequences of their work are reflected in the Civil Service of today. By removing the influence of individual ministers from appointment to the public service, Northcote–Trevelyan excluded them also by implication from most of the internal management of departments and civil service careers. The foundations were thus laid of a politically impartial, incorrupt, permanent body of officials, recruited on merit, and fortified — and this is crucial — by reasonable salaries and pensions, and security of tenure.

---

[3] Report on the organisation of the permanent civil service (1854).

It is important to remember, however, that the Northcote–Trevelyan reforms were not enshrined in legislation. Because civil servants were and are seen as part of the executive, their appointments were authorised by Order in Council, an exercise of prerogative power involving no Parliamentary procedure. Civil servants are still employed directly by the Crown. In recent years the civil service has been restructured, executive agencies have been created, the role of the Civil Service Commissioners has been altered and recruitment has been decentralised. I make no criticism of these changes, which were designed to modernise the public service and make it more effective. I simply point out that these are all changes which substantially modify the Northcote–Trevelyan structure, which is thought of as one of the pillars of the constitution, yet they have been carried out by the executive under prerogative powers. It is only against this background that the current debate over the accountability to Parliament of ministers and civil servants can be fully understood.

Since civil servants are employed by the Crown, their accountability in the past has naturally been subsumed in the accountability of the most prominent Crown servants, the departmental ministers. At the dispatch box of the House of Commons, therefore, stands the Secretary of State, but behind the minister, their vanguard visible but silent in the Officials' Box, is a vast shadowy army of figures who dare not speak their names, but for whom the minister is — what? Responsible? Accountable? A ventriloquist's dummy? A scapegoat? This is the first issue I want to look at.

Ministerial Accountability

It is important at this stage to remember three aspects of this subject. First, ministerial accountability is a convention without statutory force. Second, there has never been universal agreement about the terms of that accountability. Third, there is no independent source of authority which can determine whether the convention has been observed in a given circumstance.

As the House of Commons Public Service Committee observed in its report on 'Ministerial Accountability and Responsibility', published in July this year:

> There have always been elements of ambiguity and confusion in the convention of individual ministerial responsibility.... There is no comprehensive or authoritative statement of it which has binding force, and it cannot be enforced by legal (as opposed to political) sanctions. As

a result, the way in which it is used in practice tends to be variable and inconsistent.[4]

We must also bear in mind that the concept of ministerial accountability antedates the modern party system, with its policy platform, approved candidates, Parliamentary whipping and so on. The convention has thus had to adapt itself to substantial changes during its history.

Crichel Down

Any discussion of the accountability of ministers has to lay to rest a persistent ghost, that of Crichel Down. The resignation in 1954 of the Minister of Agriculture, Sir Thomas Dugdale, because he took 'personal responsibility' for maladministration by officials about which he knew nothing, is generally held to be the test case for ministerial accountability.

The truth is rather different. In the first place, when the Crichel Down case was first raised, Dugdale was briefed and accepted the advice of his officials. More importantly, he accepted the policy — which was what the argument was all about — that the former owners of land that had been subject to compulsory purchase had no special right to buy it back when the country had no further use for it. That approach was deeply uncongenial to the majority of his own backbenchers. As Prime Minister Churchill observed at the time, resignation was necessary 'in view of the strong feelings aroused among government supporters' [5]

Dugdale therefore went, not because he impaled himself on a principle, but because support from within his own party and his ministerial colleagues was lacking. The row over the application of the policy in this particular case was so intense that a political sacrifice had to be made for the sake of the government as a whole. To use terminology which has become popular in recent years, Crichel Down was an operational matter for which Dugdale was barely responsible: but the policy was clearly his, and without the backing of his colleagues, and particularly the prime minister, he was lost.

Attempting to Define Ministerial Accountability

Even at the time, Dugdale's professed reason for resigning caused discomfort. The then permanent secretary at the Treasury, Sir Robert

---

[4] Second Report of the Public Service Committee, HC 313, 1995–6, *Ministerial Accountability and Responsibility*.

[5] I. F. Nicholson, *The Mystery of Crichel Down* (Oxford, 1986), p. 188.

Bridges, produced a view of ministerial accountability which would have
been familiar in the nineteenth century. He wrote:

> It has long been the established constitutional practice that the
> appropriate minister of the Crown is responsible to Parliament for every
> action in pursuance of [executive powers].... It follows that a civil
> servant, having no power conferred on him by Parliament, has no direct
> responsibility to Parliament and cannot be called to account by
> Parliament. His acts, indeed, are not his own. All that he does is done
> on behalf of the minister, with the minister's authority express or
> implied: the civil servant's responsibility is solely to the minister for
> what he may do as the minister's servant.[6]

So extreme a doctrine of ministerial responsibility would have been quite
palatable to Palmerston and Gladstone, but even in 1954 it caused
difficulty. Perhaps as a response, the Home Secretary, Sir David Maxwell
Fyfe, attempted to distinguish circumstances in which ministerial accountability would be limited, effectively by ignorance. In his speech on the
Crichel Down case he argued that ministerial responsibility was limited to
circumstances in which a civil servant was carrying out a ministerial order
or implementing policy decided on by a minister. If a civil servant made
mistakes, the minister had to take remedial action and 'accepts the
responsibility, although he is not personally involved'.[7] If it is a case of
maladministration of which the minister has no knowledge, he should
clear up the mess, not fall on his sword. The Bridges formulation is not
practical. How could a minister be said to be accountable for everything
done by civil servants in his name? The consequences would be absurd.
On the other hand, the Maxwell Fyfe version leaves unclear the crucial
distinction between determining a policy and implementing it. And what
does the phrase used by Maxwell Fyfe, 'accepts the responsibility', mean
in practice?

The subject has not been helped by the fixation of commentators on the
issue of resignation, which is after all only the logical extension of
accountability. It is notable that the Public Service Committee report
which I have mentioned moves from a general discussion of the nature of
accountability to a section baldly headed, 'When should a minister
resign?'

Forcing a minister to resign has little or nothing to do with rectifying
mistakes or maladministration, and much or all to do with the political
warfare between government and opposition. Yet inviting or compelling a

---

[6] Cited by Public Service Committee, op. cit. (note 4), p. xi.
[7] 530 HC Deb, c. 1285, 20 July 1954.

minister to put things right is at least as valuable a form of accountability as forcing him to resign — indeed, it is almost certainly more valuable.

The obsession with resignation has led to a good deal of logic-chopping about the nature of accountability. The discussion sometimes has an air of unreality. The government has argued that a minister is *accountable* to Parliament in the sense that he is bound to explain and justify what is done in his name by his civil servants. If he cannot justify some action or other he has a duty to rectify matters and account for his remedial actions in their turn. He is, however, only responsible, and hence potentially culpable, for matters of which he is directly aware, or, and more importantly, for the policy framework within which his officials act.

This distinction has some internal logic, although the normal senses of the words are virtually identical. Yet I am personally inclined to be wary of formulae which contort ordinary English words by forcing them into definitional straitjackets. These contortions are required by the unreality of the whole debate. Either explicitly or implicitly, discussions of ministerial accountability ascribe to Parliament a quasi-judicial function. They assume that our legislators will examine dispassionately the case made by a minister in defence of his actions, and pronounce whether or not they have confidence in him. Everyone knows that this picture is not wholly accurate. It ignores such crucial factors as the existence of highly organised political parties which are jealous of their power and reputation; party discipline vigorously enforced by whips; and the pre-eminent position of the prime minister.

The Role of the Prime Minister

The Committee on Standards in Public Life grappled with one aspect of this separation of theory and reality in its first report.[8] It seemed to us that it might be more logical to recognise explicitly the pivotal role the prime minister plays in monitoring the standards of conduct of his colleagues. In effect, the prime minister's position is a focal point for all the factors which ultimately determine a minister's future: public opinion; the views of the backbench party; and the views of colleagues.

Our recommendation that the rule book for ministers — it is called *Questions of Procedure for Ministers* — should be amended in this way was not something that the government felt able to accept, on the grounds that it made the prime minister too much of an 'invigilator and judge'.[9] In

---

[8] First Report of the Committee on Standards in Public Life, Cm 2850 (1995).

[9] Response of the Government to the First Report of the Committee on Standards in Public Life, Cm 2931 (1995).

its recent report, the House of Commons Public Service Committee
endorsed our approach, but the government maintains its position.

The Duty of Openness

It might be thought that greater clarity could be achieved by approaching
ministerial accountability via the duty of ministers to explain their actions
and policies to the House by answering questions, responding to debates,
and so on. This approach, by avoiding the resignation issue, to a certain
extent takes accountability out of the party political cockpit. It also focuses
the debate on one of the universally accepted conventions relating to
accountability: the frequent statement that ministers have a duty not to
mislead the House. One has always to be wary of formulations expressed
in the negative. What, I wonder, would the consequences be if the
injunction were, 'Ministers have a duty to tell the truth to the House'?

In any case, we now have, in the Scott Report, a detailed study of the
practical limitations of the 'not to mislead' principle. Sir Richard Scott
concluded that statements by ministers about exports to Iraq had 'failed to
discharge the obligations imposed by the constitutional principle of
ministerial accountability'.[10] The government took a different view. Thus,
although the ensuing debate was ostensibly about a particular episode in
government policy, it was in reality a test of political strength. There is
nothing surprising about this. What is surprising is the amount of ink and
paper that has been expended on trying to devise rules to make ministerial
accountability clear in such circumstances. The Public Service Committee
has suggested that the House of Commons should approve a resolution
defining the rules which should apply to ministerial openness with the
House, and would include the requirement that a minister found to have
knowingly misled the House should resign. The government has accepted
this in principle. It is possible that this might have some effect, but it would
never 'solve' the difficult cases. It is like the Lilliputians trying to tie down
Gulliver. We would be better off acknowledging that ministerial accountability is interpreted in the light of prevailing political circumstances and
avoid disappointing ourselves with its application.

The Civil Service

I would like to turn now to the civil service. As I said earlier, the classic
formulation of accountability laid down by Bridges offers civil servants,
no matter how influential they might be, no separate accountability or

---

[10] Report of the Inquiry into the export of defence equipment to Iraq, HC 115, 1995–6,
Vol. I, p. 507.

constitutional status of their own. And I noted earlier that, in a way that would seem quite remarkable to a Continental lawyer or political scientist, there is not even a Civil Service Act to give this important branch of the administrative machinery some statutory definition.

Next Steps and Accountability

The question of accountability of civil servants is perhaps best approached by considering some of the ways in which the role of civil servants has changed in recent years. There has been, if you like, a process of developing inward accountability which has had consequences for the outside world as well. Beginning in the 1980s with the Financial Management Initiative, which was intended to improve the responsibility taken by individual civil servants for expenditure, this process continued with the creation of executive agencies under the 'Next Steps' programme. By 1996 no less than two thirds of the half million or so civil servants worked in agencies or quasi-agencies. The creation of these executive agencies produced a separation between the executive and policy functions of the civil service. Agencies were separated from their parent departments and were subject to published framework agreements which set out the performance indicators which they were to achieve and the resources available to them. They were headed by chief executives, some of them recruited from outside civil service ranks, who took personal responsibility for agency operations.

The consequences of Next Steps as an exercise in management, leading to a clearer focus on service provision and the identification of performance targets and measurable outputs, are generally thought to have been beneficial. The consequences for accountability are less easy to define. In principle, the government's original position was that the doctrine of ministerial accountability remained inviolate. There had always been civil servants delivering services to the public for which the minister was accountable. That had not changed because the services were now delivered by an executive agency with a smart new logo, because its staff, including the chief executive, however recruited, remained civil servants. No one agreed with the Dugdale line, as it was conventionally understood, that failures in the service were necessarily the personal responsibility of ministers, but ultimate accountability remained at the top.

This was a brave but doomed attempt to maintain the status quo. As events have proved, there is a world of difference between the old regime and the new. In the old days, services were delivered by civil servants, anonymous and safe within the departmental bosom. There were no customers of the service, only recipients, and no standards of customer service — certainly not public ones. Nowadays, there is the executive agency, and the civil servant who runs it may well be a public figure. The most striking thing about the controversy that surrounded the Child Support Agency in its early days was that the target of public protest was just as frequently the then chief executive as the responsible minister. When the press became interested in the failings of the Prison Service Agency, the Home Secretary and the chief executive were equally held up for criticism in a way unthinkable ten or twenty years before.

This is not just a result of media pressure. Symbolically, questions to ministers concerning executive agency operations are no longer answered by politicians, but by the civil servant chief executives. In a quite extraordinary procedure, these letters are then printed in Hansard alongside the traditional replies. This innovation, which began in 1992, is even more striking than it first appears, because when ministers answer a written Parliamentary question by promising to write to the Honourable Member, that letter is not normally printed in Hansard. Agency chief executives are also accounting officers, a topic I will touch on later, although they normally remain subordinate to the main accounting officer, the permanent secretary.

It is a measure of the evolutionary traditions of the British constitution that there was never any serious consideration of how constitutional conventions and the theory of ministerial accountability might be affected by the creation of agencies. The improvement in service provision was the overriding aim: all else was subordinate. Indeed, to some at least, if the creation of agencies weakened the lines of accountability, that was all to the good: allegedly agencies took the politics out of the provision of services and left the civil servants to get on with the job. The architect of Next Steps, Sir Peter Kemp, has expressed the view that accountability should be kept in perspective: it is part of a triumvirate with value for money and service. Of course, taking the politics out of service provision was not as easy as was believed: indeed, where important public services were involved, it was impossible. We have thus arrived at a rather unsatisfactory halfway house. As I said earlier, the theory of ministerial accountability is not easy to reconcile with the reality of partisan politics. Nor is the freedom and responsibility granted to agency chief executives.

Commentators such as the constitutional historian Professor Vernon Bogdanor, have not been slow to pick up this point. He has argued that direct accountability by agency chief executives to Parliament, perhaps through the select committee system, is now called for.[11] Like any solution to difficult and complex problems, that might raise as many questions as it

---

[11] V. Bogdanor, 'Ministers, civil servants and the constitution' in *Politics and the Constitution: Essays on British Government* (Aldershot, 1996).

solved. What if a chief executive were convinced that failures in service were due to the inadequate resources made available by the minister? Should the chief executive be entitled to say so in defence of the agency's performance? For a conventional civil servant to criticise a minister in that way would be heretical: but then chief executives are not intended to be conventional civil servants. As Professor Bogdanor says, 'we cannot expect to make a managerial change of the magnitude of "Next Steps" and expect the rules relating to ministerial responsibility to remain unchanged'. Constitutional innovation has always been possible within the British system.

The Public Service Committee, in its recent report on ministerial accountability, supported this position and argued that:

> the obligation to provide full information and to explain the actions of government to Parliament means that ministers should allow civil servants to give an account to Parliament through select committees where appropriate — particularly where ministers have formally delegated functions to them, for example in the case of chief executives of executive agencies.[12]

But in its response to the Select Committee, the government stuck firmly to its long-held position, in these words:

> The government is not prepared to breach the long-standing basic principle that civil servants, including the chief executives of Next Steps agencies, give an account to Parliament on behalf of ministers whom they serve.

The response elaborates elsewhere:

> the implications of the report would be to create a shared line of direct accountability to Parliament between ministers and civil servants. The government does not accept the committee's apparent assumption that this aspect of accountability could be changed in this way whilst still maintaining the central principle of ministerial responsibility in the form recognised by both the committee and the government.[13]

This is a perfectly understandable position for ministers to take. As I explained earlier, the way in which the executive developed under

---

[12] See note 3 above.

[13] First Special Report of the Public Service Committee, 1996–7. Government response to the Second Report of the Committee on Ministerial Accountability, HC 67, 1996–7.

prerogative powers meant that its hegemony under ministerial authority was complete. Ministers are defending the status quo, which is that there is no statutory right of way. They are emphasising that they are in charge of the executive, and that whatever delegations of responsibility they may permit, for operational reasons, ultimate responsibility is theirs. They, and they alone, are accountable to Parliament. But we should not overlook the very centralist nature of this position. It brings the accountability of the executive down to one very narrow point — the answerability of a hundred ministers, or twenty Secretaries of State, to Parliament and its committees. And given that ministers must, by definition, command a majority in Parliament, the accountability which this provides is not necessarily very strong.

A major purpose of the creation of Next Steps agencies is to free ministers from the detail of operational matters. Ministers rightly seek to concentrate on major issues of policy and resources. But if accountability is only through ministers, in respect of an agency with hundreds of offices and thousands of clients, the chain is too long, the person who should be answerable — perhaps at local level — remains shielded from public view, and true accountability is weakened.

I have argued before that ministerial accountability to Parliament was long used by the British civil service as an excuse for secrecy. Officials could not reveal anything before ministers revealed it to Parliament, so little or nothing could be revealed. Ministerial accountability is now in danger of being used to slow down the growth in accountability of public servants. We all know that in recent years many services which used to be the responsibility of elected local authorities have been removed, often for good management reasons, into the hands of specialist bodies which are not elected but either are appointed by ministers or are self-appointed. These bodies are usually funded from central funds. Their chain of accountability, which used to go via the local authority to the local electorate, now goes via government departments and ministers to Parliament. In a parallel development, activities which were formerly under direct ministerial control have been devolved, again for good management reasons, into the hands of numerous appointed statutory bodies. These changes have happened in addition to the creation of Next Steps agencies. My committee has said clearly, and I say it again today, that this is a much more complex public service than ever before, and that it demands greater attention to accountability. Such accountability can only be achieved through openness, and through requiring the people who run these services on our behalf to be openly answerable. That cannot be achieved by a chain of accountability that runs upwards from literally thousands of independent or quasi-independent bodies, of varying size, structure and legal status, to a handful of ministers, laden with half a dozen or more red boxes of paperwork to take home each weekend.

Public pressure for the public services to be accountable has never been greater. The press, for all its failings, is a very powerful instrument of scrutiny, which increasingly opens up to view the public service at all levels. Problems can seldom be hushed up. Action is sought. But the right people have to be accountable. For example once again in recent weeks we have seen the Secretary of State for Education and Employment placed in the position of having to involve herself directly in the local difficulties of one or two problem schools, because the chain of accountability only links up at ministerial level. Eventually, the framework of accountability will have to change and to follow the new management and organisational structure.

The Accountability of Civil Servants

I have approached the accountability question by considering the issue as it affects agencies and other bodies outside the central core of the executive. But an obvious source of concern for ministers would be the prospect of civil servants within the central policy-making departments having an accountability separate from that of their ministers. It is hard to see a case for such a development, which would indeed bring closer the danger of a politicised civil service. But it is interesting to note that, as it happens, there is a good and long-established precedent for the direct accountability to Parliament of senior civil servants, which is not often accorded the significance it deserves. This is the post of accounting officer.

The accounting officer of the department, who is almost invariably the permanent secretary, has a specific duty to alert Parliament to expenditure which in his view is illegal or improper, and is directly answerable to the Public Accounts Committee. The post of accounting officer goes back to 1866, and it would be interesting but futile to speculate how things might have developed if it had been taken as a model for civil service accountability more generally. The power of the office was demonstrated very clearly by the report made by the accounting officer of the Overseas Development Administration over the funding of the Pergau Dam in Malaysia — and also its limits, because of course the money had long since gone by the time the matter was dealt with by the House of Commons Public Accounts Committee.

I cannot resist noting in passing that a version of the system of surcharging councillors and officers for illegal expenditure in local government used to apply to accounting officers although not, I believe, to ministers. It was formally abolished in 1981, leaving local government as the only part of the public sector in which surcharge can occur. Some have argued that there should be a duty on civil servants to be accountable to the public interest. For a civil servant to use the justification of the public interest to release government information represents a breach of confidence and may — depending on the nature of the material released — be a criminal offence. Invocation of the public interest provides no defence in law to a prosecution under the Official Secrets Act for the unauthorised disclosure of secret information. Nor should it do so. Nor would I advocate that civil servants should have a right, let alone a duty, to reveal confidential material, whatever the wishes of their superiors and ministers, if they considered it to be in the public interest. That would expose material legitimately withheld from the public to a lottery in which the administration would be at the mercy of those with over-tender or warped consciences. On the other hand, those with a legitimate concern must be allowed to 'blow the whistle' in a proper way. There is now, I am glad to say, a right of appeal for civil servants faced with a crisis of conscience to the independent Civil Service Commissioner, which was strengthened as a result of our committee's recommendations.

Encouraging civil servants to speak up, in a legitimate way, is one of the forms of accountability which have little to do with the classic ministerial accountability to Parliament, but which are nowadays becoming more important. I would like to devote a moment or two to looking at others.

External Scrutiny

In the committee's work on its first report, we identified among other issues two important elements which help to ensure good standards of conduct. One of these is openness, which we identified as one of the principles of public life which have acquired some currency subsequently. The other is 'external scrutiny' — not itself a principle, more a means to an end. I believe that both of these have an application which is wider than to conduct alone: they are both effective ways of calling the executive to account.

One form of external scrutiny is of course judicial review, with which I will be dealing in my next lecture. An administrative parallel is provided by the Ombudsman, or Parliamentary Commissioner for Administration to give him his proper title. The Ombudsman investigates cases of alleged maladministration at the invitation of Members of Parliament. The Ombudsman has been part of our system since 1967, a relatively short time in the context of the British constitution, yet that office seems already to be an integral part of the normal functioning of government. It has also been a highly successful creation. If imitation is the sincerest form of flattery, the Parliamentary Ombudsman must be flattered indeed. There are now equivalents for local government, the health service, pensions administration, social housing, banking, and no doubt many other places. The principle that an organisation should permit its decisions and practices to be reviewed by an independent expert seems today to be almost universally accepted.

Openness

As I mentioned a few moments ago, one of the seven principles of public life which our committee propounded is openness. I am tempted to say it is the fundamental principle of the seven, because without it, in this age of scepticism, public confidence in standards of conduct will not flourish. The Americans, with their gift for the memorable phrase, describe openness as 'government in the sunshine'. The extent to which openness might go is of course a subject of political dispute, with both main opposition parties promising to introduce a Freedom of Information Act if they form the government. Whatever the advantages of this approach, we should not, I believe, lose sight of the considerable progress that has been made in recent years. In the case of personal files, successive Private Members' Acts have greatly extended the availability of records to the individual citizen. That process seems likely to be extended by European pressure, ending the anomaly by which records held on computer, but not their paper equivalents, must be open.

There is a similarly varied picture when it comes to general information, with a particularly sharp contrast between local and central government. Since 1985 local government has been required by statute to make meetings and papers open. Central government offers a non-statutory code on access to information which some commentators have found insufficiently wide. Requests refused under the code are, however, subject to review by the Ombudsman, another welcome demonstration of the ubiquity of external scrutiny.

There have to be limits on openness, of course, without which the process of discussion within government would become impossible. In this context, one can reverse C. P. Scott's famous dictum and say 'facts are free but comment is sacred'. A Freedom of Information Act drafted in a way which made it difficult for civil servants to offer frank advice to ministers would not make for good government. Posterity would rightly censure us for encouraging officials to keep their advice off paper and in informal discussions. How local government copes with a much wider right of access than that is an issue which I will explore with interest when taking evidence from those who have to operate within that system.

Conclusion

In these remarks I have tried to explore some current issues relating to the accountability of the executive. I hope I have shown that, like everything else in the British constitution, the way in which the executive is to be held to account is not a fixed and immutable process. I have suggested that too much concentration on the formal accountability of ministers to Parliament may in fact obscure other forms of accountability which have an increasing importance of their own. The British constitution is in a state of flux, as it has always been, and the present-day constitutional conventions relating to accountability have as little claim to permanence as the laws of the Medes and the Persians or the divine right of Kings. The flexibility of the British constitution is its strength.

4.   Law and Public Life

Sir Stephen Sedley

In my first lecture I considered some questions which no lawyer would have any difficulty in locating within the strict notion of a constitution as the set of arrangements for the distribution and exercise of state power. But if a constitution means — as perhaps it should — the totality of arrangements that we make for ourselves as a society, it is permissible and perhaps useful to look wider.

There is a fairly obvious sense in which the law conditions or even determines, rather than simply reflects, a society's shared sense of right and wrong (or — which is not the same thing — acceptable and unacceptable). The clearest instance in our generation has been the equality legislation,[1] which has not simply placed on the statute book a prohibition against discrimination on grounds of race or gender but has contributed to a fundamental change in the common sense of what kinds of conduct and language towards one's fellow citizens are acceptable or right. This is statute law at its best — not merely dictating 'Thou shalt not' but picking up and consolidating what was an incipient and fragile change of social mood, giving it legitimacy and backing it with legal redress. We have certainly not eliminated racial and sexual discrimination, but few would dispute that things would be markedly worse without the legislation.

There is another tranche of social mood-change, however, in which legislatures have played a passive or even a negative role, and in which it has been left to the courts of law to fill the voids. Perhaps the greatest and the most shameful of such voids was the failure of Parliament over many decades to respond to a widespread sense of moral outrage by abolishing slavery. It was left to the courts, unevenly and in response only to such private law cases as came before them, to do the job that Parliament after

---

[1]   Race Relations Acts 1966, 1968 and 1976, Equal Pay Act 1970, Sex Discrimination Act 1975. Apart from the first two Race Relations Acts, these have operated by creating, in effect, a private law right not to be discriminated against on grounds of race or gender — a model now adopted by the Disability Discrimination Act 1995. The drink-driving legislation is another example.

Parliament had shirked. Students still learn that in a single magnificent decision, portrayed in paintings and engravings of the grateful slave Somersett having the shackles struck from him as his ermine-clad deliverer pronounces judgment from on high, Lord Mansfield proclaimed: 'The air of England is too pure for a slave to breathe. Let the black go free.' The truth, as usual, is less dramatic but more instructive.[2]

English law, which until well after the Norman conquest had recognised and enforced slavery,[3] no longer recognised it by the sixteenth century when a lucrative slave trade developed between West Africa and the American and Caribbean colonies. The courts of England, however, gave their sanction during the seventeenth century to slave trading, in part by accepting its legitimacy within the law of nations and therefore the law merchant, but more directly by denying the protection of the law to infidels.[4] This worked well enough, but only so long as slaves were not baptised and only in relation to contracts for their sale made overseas. In England, Holt CJ in the first decade of the eighteenth century refused to accept that slavery could be enforced in domestic law,[5] a view which was both rejected and adopted in the course of the century.[6] When, reflecting the growing public sentiment against the cruelty of the slave trade, the reformer Granville Sharp in 1771 prosecuted a man named Stapylton who had taken his runaway slave, Thomas Lewis, forcibly on board ship, the trial judge, Lord Mansfield, tried to evade the moral issue by directing the jury that the case depended simply on whether Lewis was Stapylton's property. The jury returned a verdict that Lewis was not Stapylton's property, but Mansfield

---

[2] For an excellent account of this passage of legal history, see A. Lester and G. Bindman, *Race and Law* (Penguin, 1972). What follows is largely based upon it. For the origin of the remark about the air of England, see note 9 below. The origin of 'Let the black go free' seems to be Sir A.T. Denning's 1949 Hamlyn Lectures.

[3] About one in ten of the persons recorded in the Domesday Book was a slave.

[4] *Butts* v *Penny* (1677) 2 Lev 201.

[5] *Smith* v *Gould* (1706) 2 Salk 666. Five years earlier, albeit enforcing a contract made in Virginia, Holt had said 'As soon as a Negro comes into England he becomes free'.

[6] As Attorney-General, Philip Yorke in 1729 assured a group of West Indian slaveowners that slavery was legal in England, and twenty years later, as Lord Hardwicke, reasserted this view from the bench: 'I have no doubt that trover will lie for a Negro slave: it is as much property as any other thing': *Pearne* v *Lisle* (1749) Amb 75. He refused to follow Holt CJ on the interesting ground that if the law of England made a slave free in England, it necessarily did so in Jamaica too. He went on to recount that as Solicitor-General he and Lord Talbot, then Attorney-General, had made it possible to baptise slaves by advising that baptism would not alter their status. In *Shanley* v *Harvey* (1762) 2 Eden 126, on the other hand, Lord Henley LC followed Holt in holding that a Negro, once in England, had the protection of habeas corpus and of the law of tort: 'As soon as a man sets foot on English ground he is free'.

refused to give it effect. Within a year Granville Sharp had returned to Lord Mansfield's court with the case of James Somersett,[7] another runaway slave who had been taken by force to a vessel moored in the Thames bound for Jamaica. Mansfield this time grasped the nettle with the strength of popular feeling — though for some reason without mentioning the earlier authorities to the same effect which had been drawn to his attention. 'The state of slavery,' he held, 'is of such a nature that it is incapable of being introduced on any reason, moral or political, but only by positive law.... Whatever inconveniences, therefore, may follow from the decision, I cannot say this case is allowed or approved by the laws of England; and therefore the black must be discharged.' Although the decision had been long anticipated by that of Holt CJ, history — encouraged, by the 1770s, by a strong abolitionist lobby which found it useful to elevate Mansfield's reluctant judgment into a new turning point — has given Mansfield the credit he desired; and it has generously forgotten that Mansfield himself went on in a subsequent decision[8] to enforce work without pay upon a slave brought here from the colonies.

Before the end of the Napoleonic wars Parliament had prohibited trading in slaves, but the status of existing slaves in the colonies remained in contention. It was the avowed abolitionist, Lord Stowell, in the case of the *Slave Grace* in 1827 who, refusing to hold that slavery in the colonies was now contrary to public policy, pointed up the insularity of the decision in *Somersett*'s case and insisted that it was for Parliament to expiate the guilt which still rested upon Britain for the trade in slaves throughout its colonies.[9] Six years later Parliament abolished the institution of slavery throughout Britain's empire.[10]

The history of slavery and the common law is therefore not the story of unflinching moral rectitude which is regularly associated with the cases of

---

[7] (1772) 20 St Tr 1. In Scotland the same outcome was reached in *Knight* v *Wedderburn* (1778) Mor 145.

[8] *Inhabitants of Thames Ditton* (1785) 4 Doug KB 229.

[9] (1827) 2 St Tr NS 273. It was in the course of his sarcastic commentary on Mansfield's jurisprudence that Stowell summarised it as being that 'the air of our island is too pure for slavery to breathe in'. But contrary to legend, the phrase is not Mansfield's at all. Neither is it Stowell's. It appears to originate in, of all places, Star Chamber, where in 1569 'one Cartwright brought a slave from Russia and would scourge him cruelly, for which he was questioned, and it was resolved, that England was to pure an ayr for slaves to breath in....' (John Lilburne, *A true relation to the material passages of Lieut. Col. John Lilburne's sufferings*, 1645). Somersett's counsel, Hargrave, cited Cartwright's case in his argument, quoting this dictum and citing historical authority to support Lilburne's use of it. It is from the report of Hargrave's argument at 11 St Tr 344, col. 2, that Stowell must have taken it.

[10] Slavery Abolition Act 1833, emancipating all slaves in the Crown's dominions from 1 August 1834.

the slaves James Somersett and Grace. The common law's true claim to the moral high ground lies two generations before the waverings of first Mansfield and then Stowell, when in the first years of the eighteenth century that good judge Sir John Holt said all that the law could say about personal freedom, qualified in its territorial reach but handsomely unqualified by race or religion, until such time as Parliament was prepared to follow suit in the colonies.

But the courts cannot claim a consistent history of either carrying out Parliament's progressive measures or, where Parliament falters, doing the right thing unprompted. The English judges rejected the repeated opportunities which came before them during the worst years of the game laws to outlaw spring guns and mantraps by penalising the landowners or the gamekeepers who set them[11] — in contrast to the Scots' judiciary, who upheld the conviction of the Earl of Home's gamekeeper for murder by the setting of a spring gun, refusing to look at a contrary opinion of the English Attorney-General.[12] And it has to be said that on more than one occasion in the past they went to the point of perversity to frustrate Parliament's intentions. One of the episodes now largely forgotten by legal history — perhaps out of a proper sense of embarrassment — is the line of so-called 'persons cases' by which the courts of this country (along with those of the US, Canada, South Africa and elsewhere, it is true) consistently obstructed the extension to women of university education, entry into the professions, the electoral franchise and access to elected office.

In 1869 Sophia Jex-Blake and six women colleagues persuaded Edinburgh University to change its regulations to admit women to lectures in medicine. The prospect that they would in due course graduate and enter the medical profession, into which so far only Elizabeth Blackwell (who had qualified in America) and Elizabeth Garrett (who had slipped in through a loophole) had made their way, created a furore of academic resistance. The university reneged on its own regulations,[13] and when the women brought proceedings in the Court of Session to establish their entitlement to attend mixed classes, be examined and graduate, the university contended that its own regulations were *ultra vires*. A bare

---

[11] E.g., *Ilott* v *Wilkes* (1820) 3 B & Ald 304.

[12] See E.S. Turner, *Roads to Ruin* (1950), ch. 1, for a readable account of this passage in the law's history and of Lord Suffield's long campaign to outlaw these devices.

[13] Prompting the Liverpool law teacher Blease to remark that there are none so resolute as those who repent of a courageous action (quoted in A. Sachs and J.H. Wilson, *Sexism and the Law* (1978), p. 5 — a book to which I am indebted for much of what follows).

majority of the 12 judges who heard the case on appeal agreed with it.[14] The rationale of the Scottish decision was that the historic purpose of the university was to educate young men, and that the university itself could not by a simple rule-change make it otherwise.

When one considers the weight of condescension and assumption against which Sophia Jex-Blake and her colleagues were pitting themselves, it is remarkable that they came within two judicial votes of victory. But it was Parliament which then took up the running, both responding to and augmenting the pressure for women's emancipation. The second great Reform Act of 1867 had extended the Parliamentary franchise to all householders. The word used in the key section of the Act was 'man'; John Stuart Mill's proposal to amend it to 'person' was rejected on a vote. When it was pointed out on the floor of the House that Parliament's own Interpretation Act[15] in any case deemed all words importing the masculine gender to include females unless the contrary was expressly provided, Disraeli, speaking for the government, replied darkly that it would be a matter for 'the gentlemen of the long robe' — the judges — but that he doubted whether they would agree that it applied to the Reform Act. He was right. When local revising officers struck out the names of the thousands of female householders who put their names on the electoral register, a number of them sought to exercise the right of any 'person aggrieved' by such a decision to challenge it in court. In one group of cases the court held that the women had no *locus*, since they were not persons and so could not be persons aggrieved. In the main case[16] the High Court held that the legislative presumption that 'man' in the Reform Act included 'woman' was not sufficient to change the historical fact that at common law women had never been allowed to vote. Nobody needed

---

[14] *Jex-Blake* v *Edinburgh University Senatus* (1873) 11 M 784. One of the majority, Lord Neaves, drew support from '[t]he rules of London University, with its advanced notions', which allowed women to study but not to graduate. The women had to comfort themselves with the dissenting judgment of Lord Deas, who offered the suggestion that to save the expense of segregated tuition a partition like the one in the chapel of Pentonville prison could be erected to keep the sexes apart in the medical faculty's classrooms.

[15] Lord Brougham's Act, 13 Vic. c. 21, 'for Shortening the Language Used in Acts of Parliament', s. 4.

[16] *Chorlton* v *Lings* (1868) LR 4 CP 374.

to refer to Disraeli's prognostication from the floor of the House.[17]

Two years after the second Reform Act, however, Parliament unambiguously gave the municipal vote to women. As to who might be elected, the legislation said simply that any fit person of full age might be; and it also said that the qualifications for being a councillor were to be the same as those for being a voter. Lady Sandhurst stood for a seat on the London County Council in 1889 and won by a clear majority. Her opponent sought a court order disqualifying her on the ground that a woman, not being a person, could not be a fit person of full age. The judge of first instance[18] applied the same reasoning as in relation to the franchise: because women had never been able to hold public office it would take clearer language than this to change things. On appeal[19] Lord Coleridge CJ[20] upheld the decision on the ground that by including women expressly in the right to vote, Parliament had implicitly excluded them from the right to stand.

Anyone, however, who now believed that, save where Parliament had spelt it out in capitals, women were not persons, was badly mistaken. Lady Sandhurst's electoral victory was shortly followed by that of another woman, Miss Cobden, who delayed taking her seat until the expiry of a period of time which put it beyond legal challenge. But she was then prosecuted under a statute that made it an offence for 'any person' to sit as a councillor without being qualified. Her argument might have been thought one of the stronger ones to come before a court:[21] having been elected and taken her seat without challenge, she could not be said to be

---

[17] But *Pepper v Hart* [1993] AC 593 was anticipated before the end of the century in a remarkable extradition case, *Re Castioni* [1891] 1 QB 147, in which leading counsel cited the Parliamentary debate on the Extradition Bill 1870, adopting John Stuart Mill's interpretation of 'crime of a political character', and Stephen J (a fierce philosophical antagonist of Mill) took the opportunity to remark that his 'late friend' Mr Mill 'had made a mistake upon the subject, probably because he was not accustomed to use language with that degree of precision which is essential to everyone who has ever had, as I have had on many occasions, to draft Acts of Parliament'.

[18] Stephen J (see previous note) — viz. Sir James Fitzjames Stephen, who counted in his own family some of the age's most remarkable women, including the photographer Julia Margaret Cameron and the writer Virginia Woolf. Ironically, in *Re Castioni* (note 17 above) Stephen J had gone on memorably to speak of Acts of Parliament: '... which although they may be easy to understand, people continually try to misunderstand, and in which therefore it is not enough to attain a degree of precision which a person reading in good faith can understand; but it is necessary to attain if possible a degree of precision which a person reading in bad faith cannot misunderstand. It is all the better if he cannot pretend to misunderstand it.'

[19] *Beresford-Hope v Lady Sandhurst* (1889) 23 QBD 79.

[20] Who as Sir John Coleridge QC had led Dr Richard Pankhurst at the Bar for the women householders in the leading municipal franchise case.

[21] *De Souza v Cobden* [1891] 1 QB 687.

unqualified; but if she *was* unqualified it was because she was a woman and so, like Lady Sandhurst, was not a person. She could therefore not be a person sitting as a councillor when unqualified, especially as the prohibition itself used the word 'he'. No, said the Master of the Rolls; this was a clear case for the application of the Interpretation Act, since there was nothing in the context to prevent it: a woman was a person for the purpose of committing the offence of taking up an office to which, because she was not a person, she had no right to be elected.

Having painted themselves into this corner by the turn of the century the judges, both on and off the bench, either could not or did not wish to get out of it. In Scotland the word 'person' in the Law Agents Act 1873 was held not to include women.[22] In England the judges as visitors of Grays Inn upheld the benchers' refusal to call Bertha Cave to the Bar on the ground that there was no precedent for doing so.[23] In Scotland the women who, in the wake of Sophia Jex-Blake, had in 1889 secured admission to Scottish universities by statute, sought to exercise the right of 'every person' registered as a graduate to vote in the university Parliamentary constituency. The Court of Session held[24] that 'person', in conformity with the unwritten constitutional law which by supposed custom confined the franchise to men, excluded women; and in the alternative that being a woman was a disqualifying legal disability. On appeal to the House of Lords[25] Lord Loreburn dug a still deeper pit for the courts by holding the legal disability of women to be so self-evident that '[i]t is incomprehensible ... that anyone acquainted with our laws or the methods by which they are ascertained can think, if indeed anyone does think, there is room for argument on such a point'. There followed in 1913 the judicial exclusion of women from the category of 'persons' entitled by the Solicitors Act 1843 to take articles.[26] Because of the legal disabilities imposed by the law on married women, the applicant's counsel conceded that only unmarried

---

[22] *Hall v Incorporated Society of Law Agents* 1901 SC 170. The decision was based on immemorial usage, notwithstanding that there was a record of Lady Crawford having appeared before the High Court in Edinburgh as an advocate as long ago as 1563, and notwithstanding the presumption of gender-inclusiveness in what was now s. 1 of the Interpretation Act 1889.

[23] A fine example of Professor Cornford's Principle of Unripe Time (F. M. Cornford *Microcosmographia Academica*, 1906). His axiom is that one should never do anything for the first time.

[24] *Nairn v St Andrews and Edinburgh University Courts* 1909 16 SLT 619.

[25] 1909 SC (HL) 10.

[26] *Bebb v Law Society* [1914] 1 Ch 286. The Solicitors Act 1843 itself contained a gender-inclusive provision. The report of the case includes the scholarly historical argument of Lord Robert Cecil KC, leading R.A.Wright (later the senior law lord), for Miss Bebb.

women could claim equality with men. The price his client paid for the concession was the remark of Phillimore LJ, giving his reasons for excluding even unmarried women from the profession, that it would be a serious inconvenience if in the middle of conducting a case a woman solicitor got married, simultaneously losing the capacity to contract and to practise. Then in 1922 Lord Birkenhead LC, determined to overset the favourable advice of a special committee of the House of Lords which had included three judicial members, set up a fresh committee and secured a decision that a hereditary peeress, Viscountess Rhondda, was disqualified by her sex from taking her seat in the House. It was only in 1929, following a generation of suffragist agitation and a full decade after Parliament had bypassed the judges by legislating in words of one syllable to give women the vote in Parliamentary elections[27] and to revoke all legal impediments upon women in public law[28] that the Privy Council, on an appeal from Canada,[29] managed to get the common law off the hook on which its domestic predecessors had consciously impaled it by the simple proposition that the word 'person' on the face of it includes both sexes and that a history of customary discrimination did not furnish a very useful gloss on that obvious meaning. But it was more than forty years after Viscountess Rhondda's case that a woman took her seat on the benches of the upper House.

This was not an isolated or aberrant line of cases. In the same period the English courts held it to be permissible for a local authority to dismiss women teachers if they got married[30] — a decision which will have seemed perfectly reasonable in its time to a great many people but which no court of public law would conceivably uphold today. The common law denied a mother any legal right to the custody, care or control of her own children; and although legislation had from 1839[31] enabled the courts to award a mother custody in limited circumstances, even the introduction by

---

[27] Representation of the People Act 1918 (limiting the vote to women aged 30 or over); Representation of the People (Equal Franchise) Act 1928.

[28] Sex Disqualification Removal Act 1919.

[29] *Edwards v A-G for Canada* [1930] AC 124. Although studiously uncritical of the English decisions, the judgment of the Privy Council, seating Canada's first woman senator, is a historic text. It includes the metaphor adopted generations later by the Canadian Supreme Court in its Charter jurisdiction of the constitution as 'a living tree, capable of growth and expansion within its natural limits' — and, the Privy Council might have added, of shedding dead wood in the process. 'Customs', said Lord Sankey LC, 'are apt to develop into traditions which are stronger than law and remain unchallenged long after the reason for them has disappeared'.

[30] *Price v Rhondda UDC* [1923] 2 Ch 372; *Short v Poole Corporation* [1926] Ch 66.

[31] Custody of Children Act 1839.

Parliament in 1925[32] of the principle that the child's welfare was to be paramount was diluted by the removal from the Bill of a provision giving mother and father equal authority in relation to their children.[33] It was not until 1973 that equal parental authority was made part of our law, and not until the passage of the Children Act 1989 that we reached the plateau on which family law seemingly now stands.

Our standards change, and with them our perceptions of the self-evident and the eternally true. The law and its standards are not, and should not be, insulated from this process. The sea change in our attitude as a society towards discrimination based on gender or marital status — both reflected and promoted, as I have suggested, by Parliamentary legislation — finds its expression in the law's concept of what rationality and contemporary standards of morality[34] will tolerate. What is, I believe, healthy is that our legal culture is now less inclined to claim private access to immutable truths and more ready to accept that legal norms are not value-free but form part of the ebb and flow of society's ideas and standards. Where law and the judges who make it become controversial is in those areas where there is no consensus and where taking any stance at all means taking sides. The 'persons cases' are an awkward example of the courts taking the role of King Canute. Their epitaph was unknowingly written by one of their most passionate supporters, Professor Albert Venn Dicey, who considered the conclusive argument against giving women the vote to be that logically 'it means that Englishwomen should share the jury box and sit on the judicial bench'.[35] History has happily proved him right.

But there are creditable examples of the courts accepting a responsibility for thinking through and deciding difficult issues which Parliament is not able or willing to handle. I have mentioned the somewhat convoluted history of the courts' resistance to slavery; but a sharper and recent example is the engagement of the courts with the problem of life and death surrounding the young victim of the Hillsborough disaster, Tony Bland. Not long ago it is probable that the courts of this country would have

---

[32] Guardianship of Infants Act 1925.

[33] See S.M. Cretney: '"What will the women want next?" The struggle for power within the family, 1925–1975' (1996) 112 LQR 110 for an excellent account of this chapter of legal history and of the clash of moral and social agendas which impeded reform for decades.

[34] It is sometimes forgotten that in his tabulation of the grounds of judicial review in the *CCSU* case [1985] AC 374 Lord Diplock included in the same bracket as irrationality '... a decision which is so outrageous in its defiance of logic or of accepted moral standards that no sensible person ... could have arrived at it'. The recent abandonment by the courts of the doctrine that marriage is a defence to rape (*R v R* [1992] 1 AC 599) illustrates the meeting point of changing moral standards and law.

[35] A.V. Dicey, *Law of the Constitution*, p. lxv.

declined to give an advisory opinion on whether the life support of a patient in an irreversible vegetative state could lawfully be withdrawn: they would have left the doctors to choose between maintaining life support indefinitely and taking their chance on a prosecution for murder. In the more proactive atmosphere of the 1990s, and in the absence of any relevant legislative provision or guidance, the courts undertook the task of giving a declaratory ruling.[36] All the judgments repay reading, but that of Hoffmann LJ in the Court of Appeal is a remarkable engagement, in approachable language, with profound ethical and moral issues, starting from a predicate made possible by the novelty of the question: 'This is not an area in which any difference can be allowed to exist between what is legal and what is morally right'. In the House of Lords, Lord Mustill and Lord Browne-Wilkinson went out of their way to stress that the courts were stepping into an area which it was imperative that Parliament should occupy; but Parliament has still not done so. The reason may be that some issues are too fraught and complicated, or (more cynically) too risky in terms of public response, for Parliament to engage with them; it may be that there is more pressing business; or it may be that Parliamentarians and departments of state are in fact choosing to leave the issue to a judiciary which is felt to be capable of reading and articulating a moral consensus.

Parliamentarians nevertheless have some historical justification when they talk, as they privately do, about the need to draft judge-proof statutes. The separation of powers confers sovereignty on the courts in interpreting and applying Parliament's legislation. But for every MP who complains of judges setting perverse constructions on Acts of Parliament there is a judge who complains of MPs passing laws which are unintelligible or unenforceable.[37] In 1992 the Law Lords tried to square this circle in a major constitutional case, *Pepper* v *Hart*,[38] by permitting resort to ministerial explanations given to Parliament in order to clear up intractable obscurities in statutes. In doing this the House had to assume that Parliamentary answers, usually given in committee, sometimes given

---

[36] *Airedale NHS Trust* v *Bland* [1993] AC 789.

[37] As Cyril Radcliffe KC, Lord Radcliffe was probably the leading expert at the Bar on local government law. He was often briefed against another formidable constitutional lawyer, D.N. Pritt KC. Pritt, in his last years, told me that he was once walking back to the Temple from the House of Lords where he had been arguing a point of statutory construction against Radcliffe, when he met the senior Parliamentary draftsman, who said: 'I hear you and Radcliffe have been arguing the meaning of —' and he named a section of a recent Local Government Act. 'That's right', said Pritt. 'You're arguing that it means X', said the Parliamentary draftsman, 'And Radcliffe's arguing that it means Y?' 'Yes', said Pritt. 'Well,' said the draftsman, 'you might like to know that I drafted the section, and you've both got it wrong'.

[38] [1993] AC 593.

under pressure and designed less to clarify than to persuade or mollify,[39] are a reliable guide not to meaning (since the court will be concerned with a passage that has no obvious meaning) but to collective intent. The assumption sits uneasily with what the Attorney-General, Sir Nicholas Lyell, submitted to the House in trying to dissuade it from taking this course: 'Parliament is a political forum and not an interpretative agency. Those speaking to a Bill speak as advocates and politicians: they speak for the purpose of persuasion, not interpretation.'[40]

In both pragmatic and democratic terms there is something to be said for a court whose job is to ascertain Parliament's intent getting it if possible from the horse's mouth. But it is worth taking stock of the price paid in constitutional terms for this apparent advantage. To achieve it, the courts have voluntarily surrendered a segment of their fundamental job of interpreting legislation In theory they have surrendered it to Parliament, the forum in which legislation is publicly debated. In practice they have surrendered it to the executive, for the great bulk of legislation today comes from departments of state and is piloted with departmental advice by ministers and government spokespersons through whipped majorities in both Houses. What Hansard records, and what the courts in intractable cases will now defer to, is not in any but an oblique sense a guide to the will of Parliament: Parliamentary statements are likely to reflect only the intentions of the department of state which, under ministerial tutelage, is seeking to carry its policy into legislative effect. They may be useful interpretative tie-breakers, but they are not guides to the will of a body whose members for the most part vote as they are told to.

Pepper v *Hart* raises further constitutional questions: for example, where the meaning of an impossibly obscure passage of a statutory instrument is in question,[41] why should not the minister who made it, or the official who drafted it, give evidence on affidavit of what he intended it to mean? Although there is the practical distinction that a departmental explanation is likely to be composed *ex post facto* with an eye to the issue which has arisen, there is no true difference of principle between this and an explanation given in debate in Parliament. But it would create an unacceptably obvious inversion of the relationship between judiciary and executive. The problem is in truth not soluble by judicial expedients: it

---

[39] In addition to the drafter's notes on clauses, ministers may have written or on-the-spot briefings from their senior departmental officials. But there is no way of knowing whether a minister has given an impromptu or a muddled answer which does not reflect the departmental intention.

[40] [1993] AC at 607.

[41] My personal favourite is a sentence in a departmental regulation the meaning of which I had to argue at the Bar. It contained 123 words between the subject and the verb of the main clause. Mustill LJ, with characteristic moderation, described it as Proustian.

points up a single major need — the need for Parliament to function properly as a deliberative body where, with whatever aids to scrutiny are necessary, legislation is considered by members who devote their full working time to the salaried and pensionable job to which they have been elected, and who know what it is that they are voting for or against.

It can be said with some force that there is something sacrosanct, at least in a democracy, about the separation of powers. Without it, as Montesquieu said,[42] there would be an end of everything. But separation is a misnomer: the British state to which both Montesquieu and Madison[43] looked as a model may well have furnished an attractive alternative to the absolutist monarchy from which each was seeking an escape (in Madison's case, ironically, the British colonial monarchy which domestically had been constitutionalised a century before), but neither then nor since has it been a state in which the legislative, judicial and executive powers were truly separate. Nor have they been in either France or the United States.[44] Rather these are interlocking spheres of competence, and my first lecture considered in a little detail how the judicial sphere interacts or might interact with the executive and the Parliamentary. The word 'unconstitutional' is question-begging in relation to shifts in the allocation of functions between these spheres: to the precise extent of the shift, the constitution itself changes. It can be said accordingly that since *Pepper* v *Hart* our constitution has given the last word on the meaning of opaque legislation to Parliament, at least where Parliament, having been spoken to on the point, can be said in turn to have spoken on it. Perhaps more to the point, however, it is the courts themselves which have volunteered this surrender: it has not been exacted from them by legislation, even though it has been volunteered under the duress of having to make sense of the unintelligible.

By contrast there is in my view no unconstitutional dimension to proposals to legislate for minimum sentences.[45] They are wrong for quite other reasons. The judicial responsibility for sentencing is a historical artefact, not a ground rule of the polity. It is only in recent years that it has acquired the rudiments of a scientific or even an analytical foundation. For centuries it has been Parliament which either provides for or determines

---

[42] *De l'Esprit des Lois*, Bk XI, ch. 6.

[43] See *The Federalist*, No. 47, generally believed to be Madison's work.

[44] See M. Foley, *The Silence of Constitutions* (1989), ch. 4.

[45] A different viewpoint is powerfully presented by Sir Louis Blom-Cooper and Terence Morris, 'The penalty for murder: a myth exploded' [1996] Crim LR 707: 'Mandatory penalties ... impinge upon the constitutional position of the judges in holding the balance of justice between state and citizen. The relationship between popular sentiment and the public interest is infinitely more complex. In matters of sentencing, the independence of the judiciary goes to the heart of the matter.'

how offenders are to be sentenced, in recent years with increasing frequency. (Within two decades the power to suspend prison sentences was first given and then all but taken away by Parliament.[46] Within two *years* the courts were first forbidden and then required to take an offender's whole criminal record into account.[47]) I have not heard it suggested that the *maximum* sentences which Parliament regularly prescribes are unconstitutional. The argument that Parliament has no business to be tying judges' hands with minimum sentences is a powerful but entirely pragmatic argument, founded not on constitutional bailiwicks but on the unimaginable variety of situations which regularly crop up in court and which call for great flexibility in modes of disposal. Today the argument faces a media campaign against what is perceived as over-lenient sentencing of repeat offenders, despite the Attorney-General's power to have such sentences reconsidered and, if appropriate, increased by the Court of Appeal. What is depressing is that the one solid piece of evidence of genuinely informed public opinion — the survey of jurors' views on the sentences passed in cases in which they themselves had heard the evidence,[48] which elicited relatively little criticism of sentences as over-lenient — is routinely ignored by commentators who have other fish to fry. We have serious problems about sentencing policy, largely because the purpose of sentencing is not only itself contested but has necessarily to be adjusted from case to case depending on whether the demands of punishment, rehabilitation, deterrence or mercy are the most pressing; and also, and rightly, because public perception and public confidence are more alert to this than to any other judicial function. Nobody would claim that the courts always get it right, or even that the problems are necessarily soluble. The immediate question is whether they are problems which are susceptible to a simple legislative prescription. In debating it, sight is sometimes lost of what judges are there for — to do justice according to law. There is frequently an element of tension between law and justice, and much judicial effort is spent in trying to resolve it; but those who want sentencing to be prescribed in unwise detail by law risk creating a situation in which law and justice are not on speaking terms.

---

[46] Powers of Criminal Courts Act 1973, s. 22; Criminal Justice Act 1991, s. 5.

[47] Criminal Justice Act 1991, s. 29; Criminal Justice Act 1993, s. 66(6).

[48] See M. Zander and P. Henderson, *Crown Court Study* (Royal Commission on Criminal Justice, Research Study No. 19) (1993), para. 8.8.3. The actual question was whether the sentence was broadly what they had expected in the light of the evidence — not an appreciably different question from whether they thought it was a fair sentence. About one third thought it was; one third had had no prior view; and the remaining third was divided between those who thought the sentence too high and those who thought it too low. This is hardly a vote of no public confidence.

True, it can be said that anything which rearranges or reallocates responsibility under an unwritten constitution merely changes and never violates it. It can even be said of that most prescriptive of instruments, the Constitution of the United States, of which — early in his career — the future Chief Justice Hughes remarked: 'The Constitution is whatever the judges say it is', and which has over the years yielded a kaleidoscope of answers to recurrent questions. But there can, I would argue, come a point in even an organic constitution at which change has to be acknowledged to be contrary to the ground rules and — if it is to legitimated — addressed and debated as such. There is a respectable viewpoint that *Pepper* v *Hart* is of this class, though for reasons I have put forward it may have to be regarded as a special case of voluntary surrender. A perhaps stronger candidate for the description 'unconstitutional' is a provision of the social security legislation which was recently considered on appeal by the House of Lords.[49]

Like any other self-contained system of adjudication under statutory powers, the social security system ought to abide by the law: indeed one might say that the rule of law otherwise has little meaning. The legislation itself provides for difficult points of law to go before commissioners who are experienced lawyers and then on, if necessary, to the Court of Appeal and the House of Lords. Sometimes it turns out on appeal that benefit which has been refused in a large number of cases ought to have been paid to the claimants. The only immediate beneficiary is the single successful appellant; but provided a mechanism of review is there — and in the social security system it is — people who were refused benefit in earlier cases can in principle ask for the refusals to be reviewed in the light of the law as it is now known to be. The Department of Social Security has secured legislation in recent years which provides that any such review 'shall be determined as if the [later] decision had been found by the commissioner or court in question not to have been erroneous in point of law'.[50] Thus, as Lord Slynn explained it in the House of Lords, 'where a decision is taken by a commissioner or by a court that a decision of an adjudicating authority is wrong in law, the assumption is to be made in other cases (contrary to the fact) that the adjudicating authority's decision was correct in law'. Their Lordships went on to hold that this artificial presumption that law enacted by or with the authority of Parliament can be definitively misinterpreted by adjudicating officials bound not only other adjudicators on review but the commissioners and the courts too. Such a provision, it

---

[49] *Bate* v *Chief Adjudication Officer* [1996] 1 WLR 814.

[50] Social Security Act 1975, s. 104(7) and (8), inserted by the Social Security Act 1990, sch. 6, para. 7(1). See now the Social Security Administration Act 1992, ss. 25(2), 69(1) and (2).

might be thought, is an invasion by Parliament (assuming as one must that Parliament appreciated what it was doing) of the constitutional function of the courts not only to interpret legislation but to have their interpretation respected and given effect. It is one thing — itself a contentious thing — for the courts voluntarily to surrender a portion of their sovereignty to Parliament in the interests of clarity of construction; it is another for Parliament prospectively to overset the courts' construction of a social security measure, not by legislative or departmental amendment of the measure but by insulating an inferior tribunal's error from correction in accordance with the law. This, I respectfully suggest, is truly unconstitutional: it subverts the role of the commissioners and the courts as the unique forum of statutory construction. Instead of exercising its uncontested power to change the substantive law, whether directly or by delegation and whether prospectively or retrospectively, the legislative power of Parliament has been used in a particular class of case to reduce the interpretative function of the courts to tokenism, replacing it with a new legal category (which Kafka would have appreciated) of irrebuttable adjudicative error.[51] This is a step beyond the 'Henry VIII' clauses by which Parliament has over many years devolved to ministers the power to amend primary legislation, and which a former Chief Justice, Lord Hewart, earlier this century characterised as the use of a dispensing power familiar to the Stuart monarchs.[52]

---

[51] The judgments of the Court of Appeal (Glidewell, Mann and Millett LJJ; transcript CA.94.1565; unreported) make an instructive contrast, although having been overruled they are of historical interest only. Millett LJ, with whom the other members of the court agreed, said: '... on the construction for which the Secretary of State contends, the subsection would evidently contemplate this court being compelled to reach a conclusion contrary not only to a decision of the House of Lords but to a decision of the European Court of Justice. Parliament cannot have intended that; and if it did, this court would have no alternative but to disobey. In my judgment the construction placed on subsection (8) by the commissioner in the present case is not only unwarranted by the wording of the subsection but is unacceptable in its effect and capricious in its application. It deprives a claimant of her just entitlement by perpetuating an error of law, if necessary in the teeth of a decision of the House of Lords or the European Court, but only where an incorrect decision of an adjudicating officer has been reversed and not where a correct decision has been upheld.' The word 'unconstitutional' does not, however, appear in any of the judgments.

[52] *The New Despotism* (1929). Hewart cites among other examples the Rating and Valuation Act 1925, which gave the minister power by Order to remove 'any difficulty' in the operation of the Act. Cf: 'If this court had ... decided to quash this order as having been made *ultra vires*, the minister might tomorrow, under the provisions of s. 67, have arrived at the same end by making an order and removing the difficulty': *R v Minister of Housing, ex parte Wortley RDC* [1927] 2 KB 229. My next lecture looks at a major resurgence of the Henry VIII clause — Parts I and II of the Deregulation and Contracting Out Act 1994.

The bypassing of Parliament and the courts in favour of executive discretion is now finding an echo in a novel doctrine of law without legality — that is to say the enactment of a system which, though necessarily statute-based, is to be cut free in its operation from any legal supervision or adjudication, whether internal or external. The ambition itself is not new. Parliament spent much of the mid-nineteenth century passing 'no certiorari' clauses — I looked at them briefly in my first lecture — to prevent its boards and commissions from being tied up with litigation on behalf of vested interests. The courts' response, rooted in the 'justice of the common law', was reiterated in modern times in the landmark *Anisminic* decision[53] that no statutory body had power to go wrong in law, that error of law nullified a decision and that a void decision could not logically enjoy the protection of a no-certiorari clause. Although a few such privative clauses have been enacted since then[54] they have not been tested in court. But the coming reconstruction of the social security system may bring something different. Consider this recent departmental publication, initiating the current review:

> But the law does not just specify rules of entitlement. It also lays down many of the *procedures* by which benefits must be delivered. This has two effects. First, administrative matters end up being specified by the courts, often in ways never envisaged by Parliament. And second, procedures become petrified in inefficient routines. My ... proposition is therefore that laying down procedures in law is a barrier to efficient customer service. ...
>
> Fundamental to the Change Programme will be a review of the legal basis of decision making and appeals. Above all it will consider to what extent, if at all, the law needs to specify the procedures by which decisions must be taken. The prime interest of claimants is to obtain their full benefit entitlement, speedily — with the right to an objective review if they dispute the DSS decision. There is little advantage to claimants if their claims go through the right processes but [they] are awarded the wrong amount. Likewise it is not clear what harm is done

---

[53] *Anisminic Ltd* v *Foreign Compensation Commission* [1969] 2 AC 147.

[54] Security Service Act 1989, s. 5(4); Interception of Communications Act 1985, s. 7(8); Intelligence Services Act 1994, s. 9(4). In all three measures the prohibitive provision extends to decisions of the tribunals or commissioners about their own jurisdictions. Mandamus remains in principle available only where there has been a refusal to entertain a complaint at all. I do not know of any modern analogues of the type of provision cited by Lord Hewart in *The New Despotism* (note 52) as a favoured form of ouster clause, to the effect that 'confirmation by the Board shall be conclusive evidence that the requirements of this Act have been complied with, and that the order has been duly made and is within the power of this Act'.

if claims do not go through the right procedures but the amount awarded is nonetheless correct.

The reader glimpses a new universe, in which claimants who have not been given a chance to put their case or have been given no reasons for a decision, and so have no way of knowing what attention if any has been paid to their circumstances by the adjudication officer, appeal to tribunals who have to start again from scratch — unless the tribunals are to be likewise free to disregard all norms of procedure and to fix whatever figure appeals to them. Somewhere in this universe the 'correct amount' for each claimant will exist; but since there will be no tedious procedures for arriving at it, there will be no way of knowing when it has been reached. It was a relief to find that this Arcadia of government beyond law did not appear in the text of the Green Paper[55] to which the passage I have quoted formed an annex, and that something more recognisably constitutional is likely to accompany the rationalisation of the administration of social security. In fact the Green Paper was reassuring: if its proposal that an appeal body 'should have the scope to correct its own wrong decisions without the need for referral to the commissioners' is taken seriously it might mean repealing the unconstitutional provisions of the present legislation which I have been considering.

It is perfectly understandable that with impermanent and penetrable boundaries to the theoretically separate powers of the courts and Parliament there should be occasional border incidents and a measure of mutual sensitivity. These do not contradict the presence of a generally stable and functional system. What I have suggested so far in these lectures is that although the courts cannot claim an unbroken history of loyally implementing Parliament's measures, they have stood as firm as legislation has permitted on the role of the justice of the common law in a democracy. I have suggested too that such cause as Parliamentarians have for anxiety about what the courts will make of their legislation does not justify the erosion by Parliament, or more precisely by the ministers and departments on which Parliament depends, of the constitutional role of the courts as the arbiters of legality. History suggests that any Parliament which creates pockets of arbitrary power for executive government is taking risks with not only the courts' but its own status.

Real life, for the rest, can be relied on to go on throwing up problems which Parliaments either cannot or will not resolve. Not every such problem is justiciable, and not every justiciable problem can be satisfactorily answered by legal reasoning. The case of Tony Bland illustrates all

---

[55] Cm 3328.

of this; but it also demonstrates a perhaps new barometric quality in the courts' responsiveness to public issues, and in doing so it enhances, I suggest, the case for the courts of common law as an indispensable element in the continual remaking of our constitution in the broad as well as the narrow sense that I have tried to describe.

5.   The Judiciary

Rt Hon Lord Nolan

Discussions about the constitutional role of the judiciary tend to concentrate upon the trend of decisions in the High Court, the Court of Appeal, and the House of Lords. I shall come to those subjects later in this lecture, but I want to begin with the simpler and more fundamental topic of trial by jury. I do so for two reasons. The first is that the jury is an essential part of the judiciary. All major criminal trials are decided by juries (just as all minor criminal trials, except for those dealt with by the relatively small number of stipendiary magistrates, are decided by lay justices of the peace).

Why do we need juries as well as judges? The task of the jury is to decide what are the facts, but judges too are perfectly well able to decide questions of fact, and spend most of their time doing so in civil cases. The 'Diplock' courts in Northern Ireland, in which terrorist cases are tried by judges alone, are generally accepted as having functioned well. In his report following his Inquiry into Legislation against Terrorism, Lord Lloyd said of the Diplock courts that 'there has been nothing but praise for the way in which the judges have discharged their responsibilities'.[1] They were set up because of the fear that individual jurors could not be relied upon to deliver a true verdict, because they were either prejudiced or intimidated. The same fears have arisen in a number of cases on the mainland of Britain, not only in terrorist trials but also in trials involving other crimes of violence, and drug smuggling. And, of course, there has been much debate about the ability of juries to comprehend the issues in complicated fraud trials. But these dangers and anxieties in Great Britain have come nowhere near outweighing the importance of what Lord Devlin described in *The Judge* as the 'One really great function which a jury can discharge and which a judge cannot, and that is ... the application of a popular instead of a professional standard. To do that they must have charge of the whole case ... not of the facts only, and certainly over the

---

[1] Lord Lloyd of Berwick, Inquiry into Legislation against Terrorism, Cm 3420 (1996), p. xiii.

selection of the witnesses to be believed. They must have control of the verdict. If they lose that, they lose their *raison d'être'*. Lord Devlin continued:

> There are two reasons why they should retain it. The first is for the sake of freedom. A jury cannot fight tyranny outside the Law, but it ensures that within the Law liberty cannot be crushed.... The other reason is for the sake of contentment. People who were before content to be governed are now demanding a greater say in the management of their affairs. Through the jury the governed have a voice not only in the making of the Laws which govern them but in their application. It is good for a nation when its people feel that in the gravest matters justice belongs in part to them.[2]

I fully support Lord Devlin's view of the jury's constitutional role in administering the law and protecting our freedoms. My second reason for putting the jury at the forefront of this lecture is the crucial part which jury trials play in the education of the professional judges. For most people, the path to the Circuit Bench or the High Court Bench lies through service in the Crown Courts as an assistant recorder and then, if all is well, a fully fledged recorder, conducting jury trials of the less serious indictable offences. The Chancery judges are an exception to this rule. Their natural brilliance enables them to go straight to the Bench without the benefit of trial by jury. One of the most important tests of judicial competence is the ability to communicate with the jury — in particular, to ensure that they fully understand the trial process, and what it is that they have to decide. In a normal, well-conducted trial the verbal communication is almost entirely one-sided. The jury speaks only to deliver its verdict, and that it does in two syllables or three, as the case may be. The observant judge, or counsel or witnesses for that matter, may be able to learn a good deal from the body language of the individual jurors. Sometimes it speaks louder than words. But that is rare. As a general rule the jury remains inscrutable, and rightly so. The privacy of the juror's views about a particular case is jealously guarded in this country (though not in the United States of America). Section 8 of the Contempt of Court Act 1981 makes it an offence to obtain, disclose or solicit any particulars of statements made or opinions expressed by members of a jury in the course of their deliberations.

One of the criteria for the selection of judges employed by the Lord Chancellor, and endorsed by the Home Affairs Committee in its recent

---

[2] Lord Devlin, *The Judge* (Oxford, 1979).

report on Judicial Appointments Procedures[3] is 'an ability to handle the court', which includes the ability to control a trial, the ability to intervene when the rules are being transgressed, and the ability to sum up in a comprehensible way. It has been well said that every trial is a trial of the judge. It would be intriguing to discover the jury's opinion of particular recorders or judges, in particular cases, but section 8 of the Contempt of Court Act 1981 rules that out. It has not, however, prevented a comprehensive study in more general terms of the attitudes of juries towards the judges who conducted the trials in which they engaged, and the trial process generally. An authoritative study of this question in recent years was conducted by Professor Michael Zander, of the London School of Economics, on behalf of Lord Runciman's Royal Commission on Criminal Justice,[4] of which Professor Zander was a member, and which made its report in 1993,[5] The study was based on questionnaires administered to the main actors in every case in every Crown Court in England and Wales for a two-week period in February 1992. In anticipation of what I am to say next, I should make it clear that this was after I had ceased to be a trial judge, and had gone to the Court of Appeal. No less than 819 juries — that is, 96% of all the juries that sat during the survey period, responded to the questionnaire. For anyone interested in the jury system, the full account of the responses is fascinating, and repays careful study. I shall mention only a few items.

First, jurors were mainly very positive about the system. A third of the jurors (33%) thought that the jury system was 'very good'. Nearly half (46%) thought that it was 'good'. 15% were neutral. Only a handful (4%) thought that it was 'poor' or 'very poor'. Jurors were extremely positive about the performance of both barristers and judges. Asked what they thought about the barristers in regard to 'knowing the facts', 'putting the case across' and 'dealing with the opponent's case', the overwhelming majority thought that the barristers did 'very well' or 'well'. There were positive ratings on each of the three items from 85%–90% of jurors.

The verdict on the judges was even more positive. They were evaluated on 'keeping the proceedings under control', 'keeping a fair balance between defence and prosecution during the trial' and 'explaining things to the jury'. The proportion of jurors who thought they did 'very well' on all three was close to 90%. There were virtually no jurors who thought they did not do at least 'well'.

---

[3] Third Report of the Home Affairs Committee, HC 52, 1995–6.
[4] Report of the Royal Commission on Criminal Justice, Cm 2263 (1993).
[5] M. Zander and P. Henderson, *Crown Court Study*, Research Study No. 19, Royal Commission on Criminal Justice.

Of even more interest to my mind, is the aspect of the study already mentioned by Stephen Sedley, namely the view of the jurors upon the sentence passed by the judge in the cases where the defendant had been found guilty. Almost a third of the jurors said they thought that the sentence was broadly as they had expected, a third said that they had no expectations, whilst the other third were about equally divided between those who said it had been more severe and those who said it was less severe than they had expected.

That was the view of people who had sat through the trial, and knew all of the facts. What it amounts to is proof that the judge's view of the proper sentence fell plumb in the middle of the views held by the members of the public who made up the jury. There is surely a lesson to be learnt here by those who base their opinions of particular sentences on what they have read in the tabloids, and who suppose in consequence that the judges are out of touch with the feelings of ordinary people.

I make this point firstly because, if the judiciary really were as ignorant and insensitive as they are often portrayed, the criminal justice system would collapse, and, with it, the whole edifice of law and order. If the judges did not command the confidence of the juries who work with them in criminal trials, why should they be trusted with the very wide powers which they exercise in other areas of the law? The truth of the matter is that, up and down the country, on every working day, hundreds of cases involving the liberty of the subject are being tried fairly and competently, in open court, by judges and juries and this gets no publicity at all, for the simple reason that good news of this kind does not sell newspapers. I emphasise the point, not out of complacency nor because judges either need or expect constant praise, but because I think it of crucial importance that the judges should be trusted by the public, and I think that there is a real danger of false perceptions giving rise to mistrust, and cynicism.

Much of the responsibility for the poor publicity which judges often receive lies with the judges themselves. The legal profession in general and the judges in particular have always been bad at cultivating the art of public relations. No doubt this is partly due to the fact that, until recently, the idea of self-advertisement was anathema to the profession. Blowing your own trumpet is still a self-defeating exercise, but in recent years judges have increasingly come to recognise the need to anticipate the public reaction to controversial decisions and to cater for it in their judgment — or even, in extreme cases, by holding a press conference.

I have spoken at some length about the record of the judges in criminal cases, the area in which some of the most intemperate criticism of the judiciary has occurred, and about the recognition by the judges, albeit rather late in the day, that this criticism has reached a level which imperils the confidence of the public in the judicial process, and must therefore be countered. This I regard as an essential part of the background to any consideration of the part played by the judges in the development of administrative law. For the two central features of the discussion must be, first, the competence of the judges to deal with the problems which administrative law presents, and secondly, and equally important, the public perception of that competence.

The vast majority of criminal cases are, of course, dealt with by the circuit judges, recorders, and assistant recorders, none of whom plays any direct part in administrative law. There is, none the less, a close link between the Crown Courts, and the Crown Office of the Supreme Court of Judicature which is responsible for the judicial review cases. Almost all applications for judicial review are heard by the Queen's Bench judges, working on what is known as the Crown Office list, sitting at the Law Courts in London when they are not out on circuit conducting criminal trials. The situation is substantially the same in Scotland and Northern Ireland. Unlike their Continental colleagues administering the *droit administratif*, the judges of the United Kingdom who deal with administrative law are regularly engaged at what I might call the sharp end of the law, that is the law dealing with crime and punishment and civil disputes, the murders, the rapes and the personal injury cases.

The Home Affairs Committee, to whom I have already referred, listed legal learning, independence of mind, an ability to handle the court, maturity, and integrity as the key attributes for any professional judge. To these I would add an understanding of human nature, and of the daily concerns of ordinary people. In his evidence to the Home Affairs Committee Lord Taylor, then Lord Chief Justice, said that the judges for their part 'usually realised that the public expects them to be courteous, reasonable, approachable and patient'. So they should, and these qualities are as important in the Crown Office as they are in the Crown Court — though approachability may need to be rather more restrained in the latter. A certain amount of humility is not out of place either. Judges, after all, are entrusted with a quite extraordinary degree of power and responsibility. The powers and responsibility of an individual judge are immeasurably greater than those of an individual member of the executive or the legislature. The judge may be overruled by three other judges in the Court of Appeal, and in rare cases they in turn may be overruled by five judges in the House of Lords, but the power wielded by the judges over those involved in the cases before them and over the development of the law remains out of all proportion to the number of people exercising it. It will be small comfort to those who find this state of affairs disturbing to add that in matters of Community law the House of Lords may be overruled by yet more judges sitting in Luxembourg.

I have spoken of the demands which the system makes upon the judges. What about the demands which it makes upon those at the receiving end? The response of the civil service has been, as one would expect, immaculate. It is fully set out in the pamphlet *The Judge over your Shoulder* which was prepared by the Treasury Solicitor's Department in conjunction with the Cabinet Office, first published in 1987, and revised in May 1995. The title parodies the Orwellian notion of the executive as Big Brother, by presenting the judges as a sort of Big Brother's Big Brother, not exactly sneaking up behind the shoulders of civil servants but keeping a vigilant eye on their behaviour. The booklet subscribes to the rule of law loyally and without qualification. Thus in paragraph 3 of the Introduction we find:

> Judicial review is, as the name implies, how the courts in England and Wales supervise the way in which ministers, government departments, agencies, local authorities or other public bodies exercise their powers or carry out their duties. It is therefore merely a means (although a very powerful one) by which improper exercise of power can be remedied. It would be jumping the gun to proceed directly to an examination of judicial review and the principles of administrative law that underlie it before appreciating it is a part of the whole process of good administration.

It is hardly surprising to find a more rueful note struck in the passage of the pamphlet which deals with the *Wednesbury* test of reasonableness (*Associated Provincial Picture Houses Ltd* v *Wednesbury Corporation* [1948] 1 KB 223) that is, 'Was the decision so unreasonable that no reasonable authority could ever have come to it?', which is the only ground upon which a court can overrule an otherwise lawful exercise of administrative discretion on its merits. Paragraph 14 says:

> The *Wednesbury* test appears a very stiff one but decisions are quashed in practice more frequently than the quotation would suggest. The test is applied with hindsight, and may on occasions lead to results which may seem surprising.

It is not difficult to imagine the feelings of experienced, conscientious, fair-minded, civil servants, when their advice, accepted and acted upon by an apparently sane minister is attacked on this basis — or indeed on the other grounds upon which judicial review may be sought, such as illegality, or procedural irregularity and unfairness. Nor should one underestimate the disruption in the work of a department which an application for judicial review must almost invariably cause. Order 53 of the Rules of the Supreme Court requires such an application to be brought 'promptly', and section 31(6) of the Supreme Court Act 1981 expressly empowers the court to refuse relief where there has been undue delay in making an application for judicial review if the court considers that the granting of relief would be 'detrimental to good administration'. But the pressure on the courts is such that judicial review, which was intended to provide a speedy remedy, and which still does so in the most urgent cases, can involve litigation lasting months or even years.

Another aspect of judicial review litigation which must irritate ministers profoundly is the sort of media coverage headline 'Judge slams minister' or 'Minister was perverse, says court'. The implications in such headlines that judges are condemning the personal conduct of ministers is almost always totally false. The very large number of such headlines we have seen in the last few years has led to a recurrent theme in some of the newspapers and journals to the effect that a relationship of personal antagonism exists between judges and ministers, or alternatively that the judges have a political agenda to curb the cumulative effects of a government too long in power, to act, in other words, as another branch of Her Majesty's loyal opposition. These notions are fanciful. The truth is not nearly so interesting. Let me say something about it.

First, the judicial review procedure is primarily designed to protect ministers in government departments and other public officials from trivial or malicious or otherwise non-meritorious applications. Virtually alone amongst judicial procedures, it requires the applicant to obtain leave before he can bring his adversary to court. The requirements for obtaining leave are fairly generously framed. First, the applicant may apply on paper. This course is often followed in cases where the strength of the application speaks for itself, and the judge may be expected to be satisfied that there is a good case for leave without hearing more. If the application on paper fails, the applicant may renew it orally in the High Court or, if he wishes it, and if he feels that his application requires oral presentation, he may adopt this course straight away, without the preliminary of a paper application. If he fails on the oral application, he may renew it again, orally, in the Court of Appeal. Only if he fails to surmount each of these hurdles will he be denied the right to pursue his case further.

I should add that in some cases, either the judge or the applicant invites the proposed respondent to attend the application for leave, thus making it easier for the judge to decide whether leave should be granted, or whether there is really no case to answer. Occasionally, these hearings lead to some concession by the proposed respondent which satisfies the applicant, and puts an end to the case. The 'leave' procedure may, therefore, involve the proposed respondent in some expenditure of time and money, but much less than when a full hearing takes place.

The statistical results of the leave process in action reveal a quite startlingly high degree of success in the weeding out of hopeless cases, and thus the protection of the prospective respondents from the burden of a fully contested trial. In 1995, out of 3,604 applications for leave received, only 1,393, or 41%, were granted. In 1994, there were 3,208 applications of which 1,260, that is 37%, were granted. A number of Continental colleagues with whom I have discussed these matters have looked askance, on constitutional grounds, at a procedure which denies the applicant a full hearing, and which results in the shutting out of so many cases. I can only say that, in my experience, there has been little criticism of the system in this country. Indeed, there are many who regard it as of benefit to the applicant, since he can obtain at relatively little expense the opinion of a High Court judge as to whether he has an arguable case or not.

I should perhaps add, since so much of the media publicity has focused on a supposed conflict between the judges and the Home Office, that in immigration cases, all of which come directly or indirectly under the aegis of the Home Office, the most recent percentage figures for the grant of leave are even lower than the overall percentage, that is to say 36% in the first nine months of 1996. Of the immigration cases in which leave for a full hearing was granted in the year 1995, 47% were decided against the immigration authorities and 19% in their favour, whilst the remaining 34% were withdrawn. The corresponding figures in 1996 were 32% against the immigration authorities, 15% in their favour and 52% withdrawn. Bearing in mind the extreme complexity of the laws governing immigration, I do not think that these figures can be regarded as either surprising or disturbing. One might wish for a state of affairs in which the Home Office and other government departments and officials made fewer mistakes, but one would be a little concerned by a set of decisions in which the authorities were always, or almost always, successful. The percentage in which they fail seems to me to show no more than that the courts impose high standards, which is as it should be. It provides no basis for a suspicion of judicial anti-government bias.

Nor, in any event, is there any basis for suggesting nowadays that judges are either for or against any particular government, national or local. In the first half of the century there were certain instances of barrister-MPs being appointed by the prime minister straight to the Court of Appeal. The notion that, on the retirement of the Lord Chief Justice, the then serving Attorney-General was entitled to succeed him as of right was not finally dispelled until after the 1939–45 war. Even as late as the 1980s, the idea that the courts were staffed by 'Tory judges' still gained some currency.

The miners' strike of 1984–85 gave rise to a Gallup poll in February 1985, to which Professor Robert Stevens refers in *The Independence of the Judiciary* and which showed that, since June 1969, the number of persons who thought the judges were influenced by the government in power had risen from 19% to 43%. But that strike, and the earlier history of the Industrial Relations Court, had placed the judges, through no fault of their wn, in the unenviable position of enforcing deeply unpopular laws upon a number of trade unions and their members. The judges were thus portrayed, unfairly, as allies of the Conservative government. Those days seem a long way away now. The relative absence of industrial strife has taken the judges out of the firing line. There is no serious suggestion of party political bias on the part of any of them, nor should there be. The legal profession knows its judges pretty well, and I can think of no appointment to the bench which has been attributed to political motives. I can think of one case in which promotion was generally thought to have been unfairly delayed because of political objection to some of the judge's decisions, but that was unique.

The judges, in other words, are in the fortunate position of being able to observe, and to be accepted by the public as observing, complete independence of government. In some countries less happy than ours, it may need great courage for a judge to decide a case against the government. In this marvellous country, all that happens if you decide a case against the government is that you get rather a good press, and very possibly promoted. I cite here the case of Brian Smedley, the judge who conducted the Matrix Churchill trial,[6] and who caused endless trouble and embarrassment for the government by requiring the disclosure of documents for which public interest immunity had been claimed. He was then a circuit judge. Promotions from the circuit bench to the High Court bench are relatively rare, but Judge Smedley became the Hon Mr Justice Smedley last year. I am told that it gave great satisfaction to the Lord Chancellor and his officials that this promotion, which in other countries might have been regarded as astonishing, caused no surprise whatever in the profession, and went virtually unnoticed by the media.

Let me add one final word to set against the idea of judicial review as a recent invention of the judges enabling them to twist the tails of ministers and take the government of the country upon themselves. Judicial review, and the principles upon which it is based, are not a recent invention. As Stephen Sedley has pointed out, the principles summarised by Lord Greene in the *Wednesbury* case are derived from decisions by the judges of Victorian days or even earlier.

---

[6] For an account of this trial see Report on the export of defence equipment to Iraq, HC 115, 1995–6, Vol. I, p. 2 and Vol. II, p. 1097.

Stephen Sedley has also mentioned the case of *M* v *Home Office*,[7] in which he was engaged as counsel for the applicant and I on the Court of Appeal, where the Home Secretary had ignored a court order requiring him to bring back an asylum seeker whom his department had deported while he was seeking the protection of the courts, and where in consequence the Home Secretary was found guilty, in his official capacity, of contempt of court. There could hardly have been a clearer illustration of the supremacy of the rule of law over the executive. I might mention, incidentally, that both Stephen Sedley and I can take pleasure in the fact that our respective roles did not rule us out of the promotion stakes. But the two points which I wished to make were first that the decision in the *M* case followed directly from the decision of the House of Lords in *Padfield* v *Minister of Agriculture* [1968] AC 997. That was the case in which an order of mandamus was made against the minister, and upheld in the Lords. Now mandamus means what it says. It does not mean *rogamus*. A court order is a court order, and deliberate disobedience of it must always be a contempt of court. The second point to make, however, is that the disobedience of the Home Secretary, although deliberate, was entirely excusable because he had been advised, wrongly, that the order was not binding upon him. He was in no way personally to blame, as was made clear by the courts at all levels. We are still very far from the state of affairs in which courts and governments would deliberately confront each other.

And as I have said it is the judges of another generation who are to be thanked for establishing the principles applied by the judges of today. *Wednesbury* in 1948, *Padfield* in 1968 and *Anisminic* in 1969 ([1969] 2 AC 147), the case which established the general ineffectiveness of statutory provisions designed to exclude the jurisdiction of the courts, were all to my mind of at least equal importance to that of any more recent decision.

Now let me try to approach some conclusions. In my previous lectures I have not hesitated to draw attention to what appears to me to be weaknesses in our system of legislation and government. What are the weaknesses of the judiciary?

Let me take counsel's opinion on the matter. In 1987 David Pannick, now one of our leading QCs, published his book *Judges* in which he conducted a perceptive review of the strength and failings of the present system. His book amounted to a call for greater openness about the working of the judicial system and greater objectivity in its appraisal, qualities which the Nolan Committee would warmly endorse. He was generally complimentary about the judges and their work but he said in his closing chapter:

---

[7] [1994] 1 AC 377.

Unless and until we treat judges as fallible human beings whose official conduct is subject to the same critical analysis as that of other organs of government, judges will remain members of a priesthood who have great powers over the rest of the community, but who are otherwise isolated from them and misunderstood by them, to their mutual disadvantage.... English judges have every reason to be proud of the quality of their performance and no reason to fear more extensive public knowledge and assessment of their work. Nevertheless, there are aspects of judicial administration — appointment, training, discipline, criticism, mysticism, and publicity — which hinder, or detract from, their ability to serve society. We need judges who are not appointed by the unassisted efforts of the Lord Chancellor and solely from the ranks of middle-aged barristers. We need judges who are trained for the job, whose conduct can be freely criticised and is subject to investigation by a Judicial Performance Commission; judges who abandon wigs, gowns, and unnecessary linguistic legalism; judges who welcome rather than shun publicity for their activities.

In the nine years since that was written, some progress has been made in these areas especially in the field of judicial training through the Judicial Studies Board. The Lord Chief Justice would like to abandon wigs: it is the public, according to the opinion polls, who oppose the suggestion. What I am sure we will continue to need is constructive appraisal coupled with a wider dissemination of fact and of informed comment in both the broadsheets and the tabloids about cases and about judges. What we must guard against is change based on ignorance or prejudice.

There are other matters of concern, not mentioned in David Pannick's book, which require urgent attention. The first is the implementation of Lord Woolf's recommendations for Access to Justice,[8] in other words for achieving justice more quickly and more cheaply. For too many people the cost of going to court is prohibitive. This is quite simply a denial of justice. It is intolerable in a free society and we have accepted it for too long. At last now the work has been done and I hope it will be put into effect.

The second matter for urgent consideration is the incorporation into our law of the European Convention on Human Rights. At present we are effectively governed by it, since as a subscriber to the Convention we are bound to obey the rulings of the European Court of Human Rights. But since it is not part of our law we have too little knowledge of Convention law and play no part in its development. All too often this has led us into embarrassing consequences and in my view must continue to do so unless

---

[8] *Access to Justice: Final Report*, Lord Woolf on the civil justice system in England and Wales (HMSO, 1996).

and until it becomes part of the law administered by our judges as well as by the European Court.

Mention of human rights leads me to my closing words which I take from the recent speech of the Lord Chief Justice to the Judicial Studies Board. He spoke of the grave concern expressed by the Special Rapporteur to the United Nations Commission on Human Rights about media reports of threats to judicial independence in this country and of controversy between the judges and the executive. The Special Rapporteur said in his report that he would be monitoring developments in the United Kingdom concerning this controversy and he added that the fact that such a controversy could arise over this very issue in a country which cradled the common law and judicial independence is hard to believe. As Lord Bingham said 'The need to guarantee judicial independence is one we should treat very seriously, not only for the health of our own country but because of the extent to which our own conduct is still seen by other countries, to an extent which may perhaps surprise us, as a model'.[9]

I am not going to go through Lord Bingham's speech in full, but I hope I may have made clear my own views and my reasons for those views in saying that I believe that the judges in this country still are independent, even though the independence is always something to be regarded as precarious as well as precious and to need constant vigilance. I will if I may though quote the final paragraph of the Lord Chief Justice in which he said:

It seems on the whole unlikely that any challenge to judicial independence in this country will be by way of frontal assault. The principle is too widely accepted, too scrupulously observed, too long-established for that. The threat is more likely to be of insidious erosion, of gradual (almost imperceptible) encroachment. Such a process we must be vigilant to detect and vigorous, if need be, to resist. But my own, perhaps unduly complacent, view is that we can at present give reassurance to the United Nations' Special Rapporteur. In the country which cradled judicial independence, the infant is alive, and well, and even — on occasion — kicking.

Well so it is and let us try to keep it so.

---

[9] Lord Chief Justice Bingham, *Judicial Independence* (Judicial Studies Board, 1996).

6. The Constitution in the Twenty-first Century

Sir Stephen Sedley

In my first two lectures I considered the role of the common law in the shaping and maintenance of the constitution as we approach the end of the twentieth century. I have touched on some of the points of friction and imbalance which have disturbed or jeopardised the sensitive relationships between legislature, courts and executive government, and between state and people. It will, I hope, be clear that I do not adopt the unblushingly self-congratulatory account of the courts' role which one can sometimes find the common law's defenders advancing; but equally that I reject the view that the courts have grown too ambitious and are impeding the democratic process by interfering in the business of government. I am concerned, for the same reasons, at the ways in which the hold which the executive and its ministers continue to have over Parliament is being used to shift an important constitutional boundary back towards administrative impenetrability. I have argued that the courts have been seeking to fulfil their constitutional role of enforcing proper standards of legality, rationality and fairness in public administration — something which logically cannot be done in a changing polity without adaptation of the received body of judge-made law and practice. The controversy about judicial review may in the end be no more than an illustration of Lord Reid's observation that people rightly want the law to be two incompatible things — adaptable and certain.[1]

There is no reason in theory why this way of running the country should not continue indefinitely. The tensions between the component elements of the state have never in three centuries reached the point of fracture; indeed, because each element depends on the others there is a governing incentive not to let it happen. If such a balance were to be broken, it would almost certainly be from outside: at its crudest, by a coup; at its most

---

[1] 'The judge as law-maker' (1972) 12 JSPTL 22.

insidious, by the absorption first of government and Parliament and then of the judiciary by an initially legitimate but unscrupulous political force. In constitutional terms this was the story both of the Soviet Union and of pre-war Germany: the turning point in each case was the collapse of free-standing political, administrative and judicial institutions into a unitary state machine controlled by a single party. No prescriptive document can stem such a tide: the Nazis simply swept the Weimar constitution aside, while Stalin's 1936 constitution was a living lie. But I have been careful to say 'almost certainly', not only because history by definition cannot repeat itself but because democracy is not like an electric light, either on or off: it can flourish, it can be cramped and distorted. Its ability to thrive is more often a question of degree than of kind.

Effective written constitutions have been those which marked a decisive break with a nation's past: that of the United States, creating a new federal system after a war of independence against the British Crown; that of the first French republic following the cataclysmic revolution of 1789; the English Bill of Rights of 1689, cementing the settlement of decades of political upheaval and civil war which had finally stifled the autocratic claims of the monarchy; the independence constitutions of former members of the Empire — India in 1947 and later the Caribbean states (albeit these were handed down from Whitehall); and most recently the new South African constitution.[2] Other independence constitutions — notably those of Britain's former African colonies — have not been proof against usurpation by autocracy or military coup. But all of these can be contrasted with the simply cosmetic constitution — created not necessarily out of cynicism but more often in an endeavour to create the appearance of national unity as a first step back from chaos, like the French constitution of 1946 which was little more than a catalogue of aims running from the left to the right of the political spectrum.

This is why it is necessary to recognise that written constitutions cannot change the world; rather it is changes in the world which have brought about the writing or rewriting of those constitutions which have thrived, while those simply slotted into an existing polity become absorbed by it and change little or nothing. But while it is necessary to acknowledge these things, it is not sufficient to do so — first because the viability of a constitution depends critically on whether the will and the means exist to enforce and adapt it; secondly because there is at least one modern example of an instrument, the Canadian Charter of Rights and Freedoms, which has not so much reflected as created major political change; and

---

[2] There is a respectable argument that the adoption in the post-war years of the European Convention on Human Rights, with its 'never again' subtext, was the first collective constitutional act of the nations which went on to sign the Treaty of Rome.

thirdly because nothing is certain until it has been attempted. In Britain the push, or perhaps the drift, towards a written constitution is becoming more perceptible, partly in consequence of the work of pressure groups[3] and partly because of the promise of one of the parties contending for election to devolve powers to Scotland and Wales and to enact a bill of rights. If the monarchy decides to change its own constitutional status, a further ground will come into being.

A bill of rights is not a necessary part of a constitution: the Canadian Charter, although introduced by a Constitution Act, is free-standing, while it is a historical accident that the United States' Bill of Rights has taken the form of a series of amendments to the Constitution. But to the extent that rights are conceived — as they are in the nineteenth-century liberal paradigm to which we are heirs — as protections for the individual against the power of the state, instruments enacting them in broad and general terms have a constitutional dimension. Equally, constitutions which have no content of explicit rights can have rights read into them, as the High Court of Australia has in this decade read into the constitution's provision for a democratic franchise a personal right of free speech which can trump legislation.[4]

Perhaps the strongest reason, however, for the introduction of a written constitution is one which I have just mentioned but to which attention is not always directed: the enduring and fundamental need to keep party and state distinct. Lord Radcliffe in his 1951 Reith Lectures recalled Locke's Panglossian confidence in the responsiveness of Parliaments to the will of the people, and commented:

> It is only fair to Locke to say that, writing at the end of the seventeenth century, he did not foresee the extent to which the closely organised political party or caucus would invalidate the theory of Parliament that he was so eloquently expounding. It is a very instructive piece of our political history to note how attitudes towards organised party have changed. In the seventeenth and eighteenth centuries organised party was not respectable: it was called faction. It was regarded as unfair to the process of Parliamentary debate. ('Avoid faction', wrote Chatham's grandfather to his son, 'and never enter the House prepossessed: but attend diligently to the debate and vote according to your conscience'.)[5]

It is still the law of Parliament and a part of our constitution that an MP's vote is to be cast neither for locality nor for party but for the good of the

---

[3] See *The Constitution of the United Kingdom* (IPPR, 1991); *Britain's Constitutional Future* (Institute of Economic Affairs, 1991); *A People's Charter* (NCCL, 1991).

[4] This case is discussed below.

[5] Lord Radcliffe, *The Problem of Power*, Lecture III, p. 46.

nation and according to conscience.[6] The courts may have no jurisdiction to enforce this duty (directly at least, although I have asked in my previous lecture whether the common law cannot reach persons who attempt to seduce MPs from it), but they have had to consider whether the party system which operates very similarly in local government is lawful. In a judgment exemplifying the common law's amalgam of pragmatism and legal principle, Lord Donaldson MR held that councillors were entitled to vote according to a party whip so long as they considered, at each vote, whether their conscience compelled them to break ranks.[7] The reality which this doctrine recognises is that the grip of party remains firm in both central and local government and will do so for as long as the voting system favours single-party majorities.

Among the consequences of this is that the historic vindications of some of our fundamental freedoms by the courts of law can be reversed with relative ease. Lord Radcliffe again:

> ... such victories could never be won against the force of anything sanctioned by an Act of Parliament, because that is the final law in our courts and every judge must give effect to it. Now that the executive and the lawmaking power are to all intents and purposes the same, because both powers have fallen into the same hands, those of the ruling political party, these victories do not stand for the same kind of security as in the past. An Act of Parliament can reverse them at any moment.[8]

Have things changed in the last half century? Certainly the judicial arm of the state has become more vigilant in its attention to public administration, and the public has welcomed it. The need has been further recognised by Parliament itself, which has created the offices of Ombudsman for central and local government, giving them jurisdiction to investigate maladministration falling short of legal error but reserving questions of legal error to the courts.[9] But the domination of the legislature by a party-controlled executive has, if anything, been consolidated. Among contemporary commentators let me cite a political scientist who is also an MP:

> It is important to understand how parties have substituted for a constitution in Britain. They have filled all the vast empty spaces in the political system where a constitution should be and made the system in their own image. A hundred years ago Dicey (at least in one mood)

---

[6] Erskine May, *Parliamentary Practice*, 20th edn (1983).
[7] *R v Waltham Forest LBC, ex parte Baxter* [1988] QB 419.
[8] Op. cit. (note 5), Lecture VII, p. 102.
[9] Parliamentary Commissioner Act 1967; Local Government Act 1974, Pt III.

explained away these spaces, and the potential for arbitrary government contained within them, with reassurances that governments would only do what the electorate wanted or permitted. This doctrine was happily taken over by the organised parties of the twentieth century to sustain their governing legitimacy and embellished with further doctrine about mandates and manifestos. In this way, so the traditional arguments went, it was possible to combine the strong executive character of British government with a simple mechanism of democratic accountability, an arrangement buttressed by a political culture which completed a circle which had no need or room for elaborate constitutional rules of a more formal or entrenched kind. So the constitution was made up as we went along, with the parties doing most of the making up.

This is why the landscape of British politics is so completely dominated by party, unmentioned constitutionally yet basic to everything that moves. It underpins everything from the arrangements for political broadcasting to the selection of magistrates. Institutions and procedures of all kinds are remade in the image of party. Much of this is necessary and beneficial in achieving balance and reflecting political realities (though again, I readily concede, at the expense of minority parties who get the droppings from the carve-up). However, in other respects I believe it is profoundly debilitating in its effect on democratic politics.[10]

'Parliamentary sovereignty', the same commentator has written, 'provides a cloak of legitimacy for executive and party dominance'.[11] If this is heresy, it was shared in his last years by that most sanguine advocate of Parliamentary supremacy, Albert Venn Dicey.[12] It was shared too by Lord Scarman in his 1988 Radcliffe Lectures, and in strong terms:

We have achieved that total union of executive and legislative power which Blackstone foresaw would be productive of tyranny. . . .

---

[10] Dr Tony Wright MP in *Representation*, vol. 32, No. 117, p. 4.

[11] Tony Wright, *Citizens and Subjects* (1993), p. 6.

[12] A.V. Dicey, *Introduction to the Study of the Law of the Constitution* (1885), 8th edn, 1915, denouncing 'the admitted and increasing evil of our party system' in its manipulation through prime minister and cabinet of the Parliamentary majority in whose hands the supremacy of Parliament was held and wielded. As Ferdinand Mount points out, however, Dicey was by this time distraught at the passage by Parliament of the Home Rule Bill; and there is force in Mount's general appraisal of Dicey: 'It seems extraordinary that such an erratic and violent thinker could ever have achieved such monumental status as a constitutional authority' (*The British Constitution Now* (1992), pp. 4, 56).

> The gap ... in the existing constitution is the lack of checks and balances within the structure of our Parliamentary government and the absence of legal safeguards against the abuse of Parliamentary power. Parliamentary government has been transformed into government by the political party which by enjoying a majority in one House of Parliament has its hands on the controls of executive and legislative power.... The judges will maintain the rule of law, but cannot prevent government from changing the law, whatever the nature of the change.[13]

It may be that, at least in cases where clear evidence emerges, the courts have the jurisdiction to stop the use of governmental powers for party political ends. There is no reason in principle why an order of prohibition should not go to prevent a minister from using the facilities of his department to promote his or his party's own re-election, were such a thing ever to happen. The High Court has in recent years entertained without demur a challenge by a local authority to ministers who were using public funds to publicise what the applicant authority claimed was the political case for a controversial tax, but what government successfully contended was factual information about the effect of the tax.[14] But while the jurisdiction is, I would suggest, a salutary one, it represents no more than a fire brigade action where a clear constitutional delineation, such as we lack at present, would be a serious attempt at fire prevention. It can do nothing, it seems, any more than the Speaker of the House can, to stop such things as the use of wrecking amendments and filibustering techniques to talk out a Bill which has all-party support, even where it is done by an MP who is taking payments from a company or an industry whose activities the Bill seeks to regulate. And while, as Holt CJ observed nearly three centuries ago, 'an Act of Parliament can do no wrong, though it may do several things that look pretty odd',[15] there is nothing the courts can do in advance and little that they can do thereafter — as I illustrated in my last lecture — to prevent the erosion by statute of constitutional norms.

Judges far more distinguished than your present lecturer, reflecting on the implications of this situation for the rule of law and for fundamental rights and freedoms, have proffered solutions of two apparently very

---

[13] Lord Scarman, *The Shape of Things to Come*, the 1988 Radcliffe Lectures (Warwick University, 1989), ch.1: 'Our strange constitution', pp. 12, 16.

[14] *R v Secretary of State for the Environment, ex parte Greenwich LBC*, *The Times*, 17 May 1989. Professor Wade's concern that the leaflet had no legal force perhaps misses the point (see Wade and Forsyth, *Administrative Law*, 7th edn, pp. 595, 873).

[15] *City of London* v *Wood* (1702) 12 Mod 669, 687.

different kinds. One, advanced by Lord Woolf and by Sir John Laws,[16] is based on a fresh paradigm of constitutional law — fresh at least in this country, though familiar elsewhere. It looks beyond the Diceyan datum line of a supreme and unchallengeable Parliament and asks from where a Parliament derives its authority to legislate and to govern. It comes, they argue, from a framework of unwritten and largely unspoken but well understood principle which situates Parliament within a polity that includes independent courts of law and fundamental freedoms of which Parliament is not the donor but the trustee. This, many people think, must be right if Parliament is not simply to be the elected successor of the regal autocracy which was unseated in the course of the seventeenth century. Indeed, although the issue is posed perhaps more sharply by the present state of the nation than at any time since the coming of a universal adult franchise, the principle at stake has been recognised in this country for eight centuries or more. John of Salisbury, writing during the twelfth century, recognised that law was not an end in itself but a means to the greater end of justice, and asserted that the king as lawgiver was no more than the instrument of justice.[17] Bracton[18] famously asserted that the king, though not subject to human authority, was subject to God and the law, for it was law that made a king. It is perhaps fitting that our common law and statutory constitution, which as we enter the next millennium still possesses no formal concept of the state and continues to express all governance as that of the Crown, should carry with it the same strictures as Bracton and John of Salisbury were able to put on the Crown when it enjoyed much the same degree of power as Parliament today deploys in the Crown's name. The question is whether, as commentators from Locke onwards have contended, it is with the people alone that any final resort must lie, or whether the courts as sovereign arbiters of law have it in their power — or should have it in their power — to uphold or restore legality if Parliament should ever violate it.

The postulate of a total legal order of which Parliament forms only a part is a giant's stride towards such a system, but it does not take us the whole way. It is still necessary to demonstrate why, in such a situation, the courts have a moral or constitutional right to the final word on fundamental questions of democratic governance. In Canada the question no longer has to be asked. The 1982 Charter of Rights and Freedoms, enacted by a sovereign Parliament, has voluntarily ceded to the courts the power to

---

[16] See Lord Woolf, '*Droit public* — English style' [1995] PL 57; Sir John Laws, 'Law and democracy' [1995] PL 72.

[17] John of Salisbury, *Policraticus* (c. 1159), cited in E.H. Kantorowicz, *The King's Two Bodies, a study in mediaeval political theology* (1957), pp. 94–7.

[18] Bracton, *De Legibus et Consuetudinibus Angliae*, fo. 5b.

decide whether Parliament's enactments are consistent with the Charter
and to strike them down if they are not. It has even required the courts to
test the constitutionality of a measure which restricts Charter rights by
deciding whether the restriction 'can be demonstrably justified in a free
and democratic society'.[19] It is hard to think of a more open invitation to
make political judgments; and yet the Canadian Supreme Court has
developed in little more than ten years a lawyerlike and sophisticated
jurisprudence of constitutional adjudication. It has also been heavily
criticised, as has the Charter itself, for switching the mass political
processes of a democracy into the fragmented and mercenary business of
litigation.[20] Both things may, however, be true.

It is not always remembered that the United States Constitution, by
contrast, nowhere accords to the courts a power of judicial review of
legislation. The power was derived by the Supreme Court itself[21] from the
simple fact that a constitution which contained a Bill of Rights couched in
language commanding or forbidding Congress to legislate to particular
ends had to be enforced by somebody, who could only be the courts of law.
The logic has seemed inexorable to Americans since then. It has also
furnished a model for the High Court of Australia, which during the 1990s
has embarked on a remarkable process of constitutional adjudication with
practically no visible means of support in an elderly constitution which,
apart from providing for parliamentary government, says nothing at all
about fundamental rights and freedoms. The High Court has held that
parliamentary government is necessarily premised upon a franchise of
citizens who are free to exchange and debate ideas. So far so good. But
when the Australian parliament passed a law not unlike our own
Representation of the People Acts, preserving full and free media
coverage of election issues and guaranteeing free airtime for all parties,
but forbidding those with the money to do so from buying up television
advertising to promote one or other party's cause, the High Court struck it
down as unconstitutional.[22] Its reasoning was that the limitation was an
undemocratic fetter on free speech. It echoed a series of decisions by
which the United States Supreme Court has struck down repeated
legislative attempts to produce a more level electoral playing field by
limiting expenditure on election campaigns. These decisions in turn have
contributed to a body of law which has allowed the First Amendment (the
right of free speech) to dominate American life, rendering the protection

---

[19] Constitution Act 1982, sch. B: The Canadian Charter of Rights and Freedoms, s. 1.

[20] M. Mandel, *The Charter of Rights and the Legalisation of Politics in Canada* (1989).

[21] *Marbury* v *Madison* (1803) 5 US (1 Cranch) 137.

[22] *Australian Capital TV Pty Ltd* v *The Commonwealth* (1992) 177 CLR 106.

of the law of libel almost worthless and — most recently — prompting a Californian court to grant public access to executions.[23]

This is no doubt one tenable view of what free speech implies. But it is certainly not the only one. A viewpoint of at least equal cogency is that freedom of expression in a world of electronic mass communication is not the same thing as the traditional freedom to express your views from a soapbox in a public park; that freedom of expression has an organic link with freedom of information; and that the power enjoyed by those relatively few individuals and interests with access to the media of mass communication and mass persuasion must respect the right of others not to be overwhelmed with the views of the already powerful or fed a one-sided or distorted view of things — in other words, must respect their right to information. If a parliament legislates to this end, however controversially, can a court substitute its view of free speech for theirs without both trespassing into the domain of politics and jeopardising its claim to legal objectivity?

Those who argue for the assumption by the English courts of a power to review legislation on grounds of fundamental principle have, it seems to me, to be able either to justify the course taken by the High Court of Australia in legal terms or to offer some guarantee that the same thing could not happen here. It is a different thing if, as in Canada, the legislature itself hands the power to review primary legislation to the courts, or if, as in the United States, such review is the inexorable product of the constitution itself. There, for better or for worse, the courts will have the last word, although then only by explicit criteria laid down through the democratic process. But it is the Australian situation which comes closer to our own, for there the assumption of power by the court has gone well beyond what the constitution either says or implies. Free to go whichever way it chooses in territory uncharted by any constitutional text, the High Court has gone in a variety of directions, some entirely unexceptionable[24] but one at least idiosyncratic and politically contentious. It would be nice — but rash — to be able to say that, given the chance, it would not happen here.

---

[23] *California First Amendment Coalition* v *Calderon* (C96-1291 VRW), reported in the *San Francisco Daily Journal*, 4 November 1996. I am indebted to Professor Ian Loveland for this information. The plaintiffs did not get all they wanted: they wanted access for the press from the moment the condemned man or woman entered the death chamber (it was important for the public to know, said one of their attorneys, 'if the guy has to be dragged in kicking and screaming' and 'what he says before he is strapped down'), but the judge allowed access only from the inception of the process of execution. One of the plaintiffs was the American Civil Liberties Union.

[24] E.g., *Nationwide News Pty Ltd* v *Wills* (1992) 177 CLR 1.

Here therefore lies the attraction of the other approach — to put it in writing. As its most distinguished and longest-standing advocate, Lord Scarman, argued when he delivered these lectures eight years ago:

> We have no need of an American style constitution [he is referring to the separation and definition of the state's powers]: but we need to incorporate into our constitution the principle that the source of power is the people and that the powers of government are the people's powers. We need a constitutional definition of the powers of government and a declaration of those fundamental rights and liberties which it is the constitutional duty of government in all its three branches to protect and to cherish, and machinery for enforcing the duty.[25]

Inevitably one asks whether putting it all in writing is likely to be a productive solution of the problems to some of which these lectures have drawn attention. Its immediate attractions are obvious: certainty, clarity, principle. Its drawbacks are, however, almost as obvious. Such an instrument has to be negotiated with and by an infinite range of interests and viewpoints, among whom there will be the winners and losers dictated by the balance of power at the moment of enactment. Simply to put in writing our arrangements for the distribution and exercise of state power at a point of history where no comprehensive new consensus has emerged is to risk consolidating state power wherever it happens at that moment to reside. Constitution-making is for life, not just for Christmas. Whatever is enacted will either become fixed for the foreseeable future if the instrument is entrenched or will be variable, if it is not entrenched, at the whim of succeeding Parliaments. As 1996 draws to a close, however, it may be unwise to look too far down this road, because there is at least a possibility that within a year limited constitutional reform will be under way, involving the devolution of as yet unspecified powers to Scotland and Wales and the incorporation of the European Convention on Human Rights as a first step towards a domestic bill of rights. None of this is certain; but it provides a practical focus for the remainder of what I have to say.

Although Lord Scarman did not consider it necessary to adjust the separation of powers, others think it is. Very recently Lord Steyn has added his weight to the argument that the office of Lord Chancellor, as head of a department of state and Speaker of one of the Houses of Parliament and head of the judiciary, is constitutionally untenable.[26] His proposal that the Lord Chief Justice should be head of the judiciary is simple enough, but it would mean that instead of relying on the resources of a department of

---

[25] Lord Scarman, op. cit. (note 13), p. 17
[26] Lord Steyn, annual Administrative Law Bar Association lecture, 27 November 1996.

state the judiciary would have to have — as it does in the United States — a full apparatus of self-government. Any such apparatus requires a budget, and the source of any such budget must be public funds. Either, therefore, the system of justice must be self-financing through court fees and the like, or the Treasury must continue to fund it. Both schemes have evident drawbacks, but the question and its solution are critical for the future independence of the judiciary.

A similar question, as many commentators have pointed out, hangs over the office of Attorney-General. How feasible is it in reality to take important decisions about prosecutions or to give advice solely in the public interest when the decision-maker is a member of the government and inevitably sensitive also to its interests? It is only if those two interests are the same thing (as the jury which tried Clive Ponting was directed they were) that the problem disappears. But to postulate this is to take the fundamental risk of substituting party for state. The constitution we bequeathed to India took no such risk: it made the office of Attorney-General independent of government. Not long after independence it was amended to permit the holder of the office to address parliament. Can it be that difficult to think of doing the same for ourselves?

Opinion polls on the question of a bill of rights seem consistently to indicate a desire for change. What they do not and cannot answer are the questions: what bill and what rights?

If anything is to be passed into our law swiftly and uncontroversially, it will have to be the European Convention on Human Rights. The Convention, which will soon be half a century old, is showing both its age and its durability; in any event, it is all we have. We do not know whether it will be enacted on the New Zealand model,[27] as a simple gloss on such legislation as will tolerate it, or entrenched on the Canadian model as a governing set of standards to which legislation must yield unless Parliament has expressly overridden the bill of rights itself. Each model continues to give the legislature the last word; but each compels the lawmaker to face the opprobrium of seeking to maintain legislation in the face of an argument or an adjudication that it violates fundamental rights or freedoms. The differences may in the end be differences of degree rather than of kind, especially if our courts show the will shown by the New Zealand Court of Appeal under the presidency of Sir Robin Cooke[28] to invest the rights acknowledged by Parliament with remedies by which it has always been the obligation of the courts to vindicate rights.[29]

---

[27] Bill of Rights Act 1990 (NZ).

[28] Now Lord Cooke of Thorndon, sitting by virtue of his previous office as a judicial member of the House of Lords.

[29] *Simpson* v *Attorney-General (Baigent's* case) [1994] 3 NZLR 667.

But what in my view matters more is the content of a bill of rights, and even more than its content, its philosophy. The European Convention, part of the painful reconstruction of civilisation in Europe after twelve years of Nazi barbarity, looks back to the nineteenth-century liberal view of rights as shields for the individual against the power of the state. This remains a necessary part of any bill of rights for reasons which these lectures have made plain. The Convention also looks forward in part to a welfare state in which positive rights exist — the right to education for example. In doing so it anticipates a series of further calls on the state which, although they are sometimes segregated as 'social and economic' rights, are today arguably just as real. Lord Radcliffe in his Reith Lectures, delivered the year after the Convention was drafted, included in our fundamental rights 'the bundle of rights that depend on National Insurance' even though these were entirely Parliamentary and very recent in origin.[30] Given the inclusion of education in the European Convention, it is difficult to maintain a classification of fundamental rights which excludes those that call on the state to fund them; yet it is equally difficult to erect a battery of such rights which only a state with both the necessary wealth and the necessary inclination could deliver. This is a function of future debate which, I would suggest, will start from rather than stop with the enactment of the Convention.

Once such a debate is under way, fundamental questions are thrown up. Ought we to recognise a basic right to live free of fear? A right to a wholesome environment? A right to health care? Rights to food and shelter — which are arguably more basic than even the right to education? A right to information? None of these is excluded by the philosophy of rights, but none of them finds a place in the European Convention, simply because they did not seem to the framers to be necessary or appropriate in 1950.

Some of them can without doubt be argued for as juridical extensions of what is already in the Convention. The High Court of India, for example, has already responded to the scandal of environmental degradation in that country by reading into the constitutional right to life a right not merely not to be killed unlawfully but to enjoy tolerable environmental conditions of existence. It has also devised powerful and novel mechanisms for carrying its orders into effect. Its jurisprudence may well be a model for others. The United States Supreme Court has over a number of years dealt with abortion, which the Constitution does not mention, as an aspect of privacy, which the Constitution does not mention either but which the Court has found to be a value implicit in the Fourteenth Amendment. This

---

[30] Lord Radcliffe, op. cit. (note 5), Lecture VII, p. 102.

may be classed as the fabrication of jurisdiction, but it illustrates what I have suggested is a key judicial function: a readiness to respond to justiciable issues which legislatures will not touch or cannot agree on or — just as seriously — on which they legislate in disregard of minority interests. But equally — and the debate must address this too — there is nothing in any of the texts I have been considering to block the road taken by the High Court of Australia towards free speech for the wealthy. Are principled outcomes even more important than principled inputs; and if they are, how does an instrument based on principles seek to control outcomes, except by a final parliamentary override?

Other rights, if we are to treat them as such, throw up still more basic questions. The right of privacy, which does feature in the European Convention, was probably conceived as a right not to have the state prying into one's private life except for good and necessary reasons. But in the decades since the Convention was first signed, while the threat from the state has remained real, it is the mass media which have overtaken the state as the major threat to personal privacy. A paradigm which poses rights as shields only against the state has a limited contribution to make to the protection of individuals from the invasion of their personal space in the world of the twenty-first century. The European Court of Human Rights has attempted to keep pace with this reality by insisting on the obligation of the state not only to respect rights but to pass laws to make sure that private interests respect them too. But is it enough? Faced with a void in the Parliamentary will to legislate in defence of privacy, distinguished lawyers, the present Lord Chief Justice among them,[31] have argued for the courts of this country to do what those of France and Germany have already done and to meet a pressing social need by introducing a tort of unjustified invasion of privacy. Indeed, in a future legal order predicated on a bill of rights, to leave it to the legislative arm of the state to regulate the activities of private interests in order to protect the rights of others may be to drain the judicial function of meaning: for where the United Kingdom comes under a treaty obligation to rectify breaches of the Convention found by the Strasbourg court to have occurred, no domestic judicial power, however sovereign, can compel an equally sovereign Parliament to legislate if it does not wish to.

---

[31] Sir Thomas Bingham, 'Should there be a law to protect personal rights of privacy?' (lecture, 1996); Lord Hoffmann, 'Mind your own business' (The 1996 Goodman Lecture); Eric Barendt, 'Privacy and the Press', *Yearbook of Media and Entertainment Law, 1995*; Basil Markesinis and Nico Nolte, 'Some comparative reflections on the right of privacy of public figures in public places', in *Extending Obligations*, ed. Birks (forthcoming 1997).

The prospective patriation of the European Convention, in other words, calls for a new and different approach to the responsibilities of state and private bodies for the violation of individual rights — especially if it is to be succeeded by a more ambitious domestic bill of rights. If it is to be meaningful, the state-versus-individual paradigm needs to make way for a concept of rights enforceable by the courts against any invasion of them from whatever quarter. This may take either or both of two forms. It may consist of a reformulation of relevant rights to make it clear that remedies are to be given for their violation whoever violates them. It may take the form of an enlargement of the state's obligation to give a remedy so as expressly to include the courts in the meaning of the state. Indeed, since the second of these two steps has a bearing on more than simply the state-and-individual issue, there is much to be said for treating them as complementary rather than alternative. There is still more to be said for beginning to regard rights not as personal possessions but as part of a pattern of social obligations.

The recognition of the courts as secondary makers of law as well as primary interpreters of it is perhaps the main thread that has run through these lectures on our constitution. I have suggested that this role has not only been historically — though not universally — respectable but continues to be important in our development and functioning as an advanced democracy. I suggest now, in closing, that the same is likely to be true in the coming years as our jurisprudence constellates with that of other nations in the common law world and on the continent of Europe, and as the individual in our society faces new pressures and threats from new sources. To the extent that Parliament is able to purge itself of the taint of corruption — the purchase of MPs' judgment and services cannot be described as anything else — and to function as a crucible of open public debate and decision-making; to the extent that it can assert its control over ministers and their departments: to this extent people will cease to have to look to the courts for protection and redress. We have inherited a civil service, one of the greatest creations of the Victorians, of high intellectual calibre and with exemplary standards of service and probity. Although by the use of prerogative power much of it has now been moved into semi-autonomous Next Steps agencies, and although the abolition of jobs for life will mean that civil servants spend more time than they should looking over their shoulders, its standards are still there to be nurtured.[32] But vigilant courts of law will never cease to be an essential element in a constitutional democracy, whether the constitution is written or, like ours

---

[32] It is too early to comment on the impact of the Deregulation and Contracting Out Act 1994 which permits far more radical changes.

at present, understood — so long, at least, as our understanding of it is a little fuller than that of Mr Podsnap:[33]

> 'And Do You Find, Sir,' pursued Mr Podsnap, with dignity, 'Many Evidences that Strike You, of our British Constitution in the Streets Of The World's Metropolis, London, Londres, London?'
>
> The foreign gentleman begged to be pardoned, but did not altogether understand. . . .
>
> 'It merely referred,' Mr Podsnap explained, with a sense of meritorious proprietorship, 'to Our Constitution, Sir. We Englishmen are Very Proud of our Constitution, Sir. It Was Bestowed Upon Us By Providence. No Other Country is so Favoured as This Country.'

Bestowed upon us by providence it may have been, but it will be by judgment, not by luck, that our protean constitution continues to serve us as well in the years to come as it has done in the past.

---

[33] Charles Dickens, *Our Mutual Friend* (Penguin edn), pp. 178–9.

7.   Postscript: The Courts, Law and Convention

Professor Geoffrey Wilson

There could be no one more appropriate to deliver the 1996–97 lectures which commemorate the name of Lord Radcliffe, the first Chancellor of the University, than Lord Nolan and Sir Stephen Sedley and no more topical subject than the future of the British constitution. Lord Nolan, besides being a Law Lord, has leapt to the public eye as chairman of the Committee on Standards in Public Life — it is even called the Nolan Committee — just as Lord Radcliffe was called on to preside over investigations into such matters as the publication of ministerial memoirs following the controversy over the publication of the diaries of Richard Crossman who had been a minister in Harold Wilson's Labour government from 1964 to 1970.[1] Sir Stephen Sedley is in the forefront of one of the major constitutional developments centred on the courts, the practice of judicial review of acts and decisions of public bodies, in particular central and local government. And the lectures come at a time when it is being said that we cannot go on as we have been going on in the past, and that it is time to look more deeply into our present arrangements to see if they need to be improved and, if so, how.

The Challenge

It is a feature of these lectures that neither lecturer opts for a written constitution as the obvious solution as Lord Scarman, another former Chancellor of the University, did in his Radcliffe lectures 'The shape of things to come' in 1988. But they do call for a rethinking of existing structures and styles and, by implication at least, raise the question whether there is indeed a halfway house between where we are now and a full-scale shift to a written constitution.

---

[1] Report of the Privy Counsellors on Ministerial Memoirs, Cmnd 6386 (1976).

That this is no mean challenge can be seen when one reminds oneself, as one must frequently do in the British context, just how strong the written tradition has become, with its emphasis on law and constitutional courts and a reliance on a written text for determining what is constitutional and what is not.

There has really been no looking back since the United States paved the way in 1787. A written constitution was one of the first demands made at the beginning of the French Revolution. It was the goal of the Germans who met at Frankfurt in 1848. It marked the beginning of the French Republic in 1875 and the first attempts of Germany to provide for a republican democratic government in Weimar in 1919. It was a written constitution that was imposed on Japan after the Second World War and it has been around the Grundgesetz of 1949 that Germany has built its new democratic government. So strong has been the trend that it looks as if it has the force of a natural law of progression. The experience of Germany since 1949 is particularly important because it presents the major polar alternative to the British experience and tradition within the European Community and it is not only therefore a competing example in principle, but may increasingly become the competing example in practice within the overall framework of the European Community and the European Union.

And Britain itself has not been without its calls to follow this tradition. Good arguments for such a change have been put forward on the basis of inadequate consensus to support the existing way of doing things, the need to protect minorities, and the desire to incorporate a bill of rights and for some form of devolution, if not federalism, all of which, it has been argued, would be facilitated by a switch to a written constitutional regime.

The Unwritten Tradition

Britain's way has so far been different. At no time (apart perhaps from the Instrument of Government of 1653) has it been felt desirable or necessary to sit down and devise a written constitution. The misleadingly named Bill of Rights of 1689 was in this respect typical. It consisted largely of a list of complaints about the behaviour of the Stuart kings and settled a number of matters which had caused controversy up till then. But neither it, nor the Act of Settlement which followed soon after, attempted to provide a comprehensive framework for the future and, if they had, it would have not been what actually happened. The transfer of power from the monarch to his ministers over the next two hundred years was not the result of any formal constitutional changes but as a result of changes in political practice which hardened into what have become known as constitutional conventions. That some of the most important of these developments were largely unforeseen is evidenced by the fact that prime minister and cabinet began as words of criticism and abuse. And not only were the developments unforeseen. Many of the changes by which power was transferred from the monarch to ministers responsible to Parliament took place almost imperceptibly and were so gradual as to make it difficult to allocate a particular date or event to them. The piecemeal tradition continued into the nineteenth and even the twentieth centuries, when major changes were made in the law. The franchise was extended in 1832, 1867, 1884, 1918 and 1929. When the House of Lords provoked a constitutional crisis by rejecting the budget proposals of the Liberal Chancellor of the Exchequer, Lloyd George, in 1909, the response was to cut down its powers in the Parliament Act 1911 (and a further reduction of its power to delay legislation was carried through in 1949). And, although British Parliamentary government came under strong attack in the 1930s as Parliamentary institutions did throughout Europe, they survived. Since the war new institutions have been created, such as the Parliamentary Commissioner for Administration (the Ombudsman) and life peers, a wider use has been made by Parliament of Select Committees, there has been an attempt to shift the burden of administration from central government departments to government agencies, but no written constitution.

In spite of the use of the law for some of the changes it still remains the case that important parts of the constitution are regulated not by law but by convention, and this remains one of its major distinguishing features. There are, it is said, legal rules and there are conventional rules, each with the same binding force but with many of the conventions not supported by legal rule and therefore not falling within the jurisdiction of the courts. What might be called the grand conventions still lie at the heart of the constitution. They underpinned the gradual transfer of powers from the monarch to her ministers, the limitation of her freedom to choose who should be her ministers, in particular the prime minister, the person who was entitled to form a government, and to dismiss ministers or dissolve Parliament, and the virtual extinction of her power to refuse assent to legislation. But it does not stop there. Conventions reach into every part of the constitution. The rules of procedure and practice of the House of Commons, which help to shape the ground rules of political debate and include provisions as regards the legislative process, the curtailment of debate, the rights of the opposition to choose the subject matter of debate, and which strike the current balance between the need for governments to be able to implement their plans and policies and the opportunities granted to the opposition not only to express their public criticism of them, but also to present themselves to the electorate as a future alternative government

— all these rest on convention. It is convention which protects them from arbitrary change and gives them their fundamental character. With none of these do the courts have any direct involvement.

Of course one must not exaggerate. It is not that British judges never have to consider matters of constitutional importance. The British constitution is a mixture of law and convention. The courts were the scene of major constitutional battles at the beginning of the seventeenth century, in *Bates', Darnel's* and *Hampden's* cases,[2] for example, though their decisions did not settle the matter, and nothing quite like them has been seen since. But questions about the prerogative which lay at the heart of the early Stuart cases have cropped up subsequently, e.g., when the House of Lords had to decide in 1917 whether the government could continue to exercise a prerogative power to occupy property for the defence of the realm after a statute had given it the necessary power, but which subjected it to a requirement to pay compensation;[3] or whether the government could go behind the grant of an air licence to Freddy Laker by the statutory body, the Civil Aviation Authority, and use its prerogative powers under a treaty to prevent him taking advantage of it by refusing to nominate him as a designated carrier to the United States;[4] or whether the government could ban the workers at the Cheltenham surveillance unit from being members of trades unions.[5] The scope of the prerogative, the fact that treaties cannot change the law or give rise to rights and duties enforceable in the courts, the supremacy of statute over prerogative, all of these rest on decisions of the courts. Applications for judicial review are particularly likely to raise questions of constitutional importance of this kind, e.g., whether a pressure group was entitled to challenge what was said to be an uneconomic use of development funds to support the financing of the Pergau Dam in Malaysia,[6] or whether a government minister could be held to be in contempt of court.[7] It is court decisions, too, which are usually cited to support the basic principle of the sovereignty of Parliament, which is the cornerstone of the relationship between government and Parliament, on the one hand, and the courts, on the other. It is the courts, too, which have recently confirmed what the European Court of Justice had claimed from the beginning, that in any conflict between British law, including

---

[2] *Attorney-General* v *Bates* (1610) 2 St Tr 371; *Darnel's* case (1627) 3 St Tr 1; *R* v *Hampden* (1637) 3 St Tr 826.

[3] *Attorney-General* v *De Keysers Royal Hotel Ltd* [1920] AC 508.

[4] *Laker Airways* v *Department of Trade* [1977] QB 643.

[5] *Council of Civil Service Unions* v *Minister for the Civil Service* [1985] AC 374.

[6] *R* v *Secretary of State for Foreign and Commonwealth Affairs, ex parte World Development Movement Ltd* [1995] 1 WLR 386; and cf. *R* v *HM Inspectorate of Pollution, ex parte Greenpeace Ltd* [1994] 1 WLR 570.

[7] *Re M* [1994] 1 AC 377.

British statute law, and European Community law British law must give way.[8]

And the contributions of British judges to the development of the constitution and constitutional principles have not been confined to what they have done in court. As Lord Nolan's present commitments illustrate, British judges are frequently called upon to make judgments on or at least make assumptions about constitutional matters outside of the courts. Lord Diplock was asked to examine the extent to which the normal judicial processes could be adapted to meet problems of intimidation and lack of co-operation of witnesses in terrorist offences; Lord Lloyd the legislation against terrorism;[9] Lord Scarman the appropriate use and behaviour of the police in policing communities and preserving and restoring public order;[10] and Lord Denning the work of the Security Services.[11] And the matters they have been called upon to look at have not been on the periphery or limited to the kind of fact finding work for which provision is made by the Tribunals of Inquiry Act 1921 such as unauthorised leaks of proposed changes in the bank rate.[12] They have been appointed to look at matters at the very heart of the constitution.

Nothing can be more striking in this respect than Sir Richard Scott's inquiry into the export of arms to Iraq.[13] For here was a judge being called upon to look among other things at the working of one of the basic grand conventions of the constitution, the doctrine of the responsibility of ministers to Parliament, an area, Parliamentary proceedings, from which the judges when sitting in court are expressly excluded by a provision of the Bill of Rights of 1689. And the same is true of Lord Nolan's work on standards in public life, which was prompted by concern about the behaviour of Members of Parliament. One sometimes sees these wider activities referred to as extra-judicial. But this is a mistake. They may take place outside of a court. But the use of judges as a resource for independent inquiry, in matters which deeply affect the way in which the government of the country works in practice, is such a regular occurrence that it is difficult to see it as extra-judicial. These are constitutional functions performed by judges precisely because they are judges, albeit not by judges sitting in court.

---

[8] *R v Secretary of State for Transport, ex parte Factortame Ltd (No. 2)* [1991] 1 AC 603.

[9] Report of the Committee on Legal Procedures to Deal with Terrorist Activities in Northern Ireland, Cmnd 5185 (1972); Report of the Inquiry into Legislation against Terrorism, Cm 3420 (1996).

[10] Report into the Red Lion Square Disorders, Cmnd 5919 (1974); Report of an Inquiry into the Disorders in Brixton, Cmnd 8427 (1981).

[11] Lord Denning's Report, Cmnd 2152 (1963).

[12] Report of the Tribunal of Inquiry into the Premature Disclosure of the Bank Rate, Cmnd 350 (1957).

[13] Report of the Inquiry into the Export of Defence Equipment to Iraq, HC 115, 1995–6.

But in spite of the involvement of judges in both the legal and the conventional aspects of the constitution, in and out of court, it remains the case that, as a result of not having a general constitutional role or a text which purports to cover the whole constitutional framework from which to work, there is no role for British judges equivalent to that of the judges of the Supreme Court of the United States, the Supreme Court of India or the German Verfassungsgericht, or, as Sir Stephen notes, more recently, the High Court of Australia or to that which Canadian courts now have in relation to the Canadian Charter of Rights and Freedoms.

British judges have not even till now had the experience of administering a bill of rights as they have not regarded the European Convention on Human Rights, of which Britain is a signatory, as a part of English law. As a result they have not had the need nor the opportunity to develop or even consider general principles of or assumptions about the constitution as a whole. Their constitutional contribution has in this respect suffered from multiple fragmentation. In practice they draw a sharp distinction between law, which they see as the natural subject matter of their concerns, and convention, and between what they do inside and what they do outside of the courts. And what they do in court is fragmented both because what is regulated by law lacks any natural unity (administrative law perhaps apart) as the division between which parts of the constitution are legal and which are not is often arbitrary and the separate parts do not always make sense in isolation, and because of their tradition of operating on a statute-by-statute, case-by-case basis, relying on or developing general principles only to the extent necessary to dispose of the particular case in front of them.

Even when they make constitutional assumptions or rely on general principles these are not usually subjected to the same critical scrutiny as the rules of law with which they deal, and, because they are not rooted in a single comprehensive text, they tend to be diffuse and even rhetorical. In this respect both lecturers are stepping outside general British judicial tradition in looking at the constitution as whole, Lord Nolan from the perspective of a judge who is at the moment engaged in the extra-court (but, as was suggested earlier, not extra-judicial) activity of heading a committee which is making suggestions for improvement in standards of public life, Sir Stephen Sedley from the perspective of a High Court judge, particularly one exercising the new administrative jurisdiction which is attempting to shake free from the shackles of the technicalities of particular remedies and the provision of particular statutes which hindered development of British administrative law in the past, and who is attempting to put these new legal developments of judicial review into a broader constitutional framework.

As with the law so with the conventions. There has been little attempt to integrate them into the single equivalent of a written constitution. The so called Commission on the Constitution[14] was a disappointment in this respect. There is no Code of Conventions. There is no single place of last resort which can give an authoritative judgment on many of the basic features of the unwritten constitution, though there are partial codes and provision has been made for some parts of it to be subject to determination and adjudication by people or institutions other than the courts.[15]

In other cases, if one wants to discover what the conventions are one will be sent to a wide variety of sources and in many cases the answer will not be conclusive. One goes for a discussion of collective responsibility to the Radcliffe report[16] (supplementing the court decision in *Attorney-General* v *Jonathan Cape Ltd* [1976] QB 752); for delegated legislation to the Committee on Ministers' Powers,[17] for tribunals and inquiries to the Franks Committee on Tribunals and Inquiries;[18] for ministerial accountability and standards in public life to the reports of Sir Richard Scott and Lord Nolan's committee. For the privileges and procedures of the House of Commons one goes to Erskine May,[19] for a definition of maladministration to the reports of the Parliamentary Commissioner and those of the Select Committee which watches over and supports his activities. Reports of Select Committees of the House of Commons and governments' responses to them are a major source, as can be seen, for example, in relation to the conventions relating to European legislation[20] and ministers and civil servants.[21] And because practice and convention go so closely

---

[14] Royal Commission on the Constitution, Cmnd 5460 (1973).

[15] It has been one of the major functions of Lord Nolan's committee to produce both codes of conduct and means for adjudicating allegations that they have been broken, reducing grey areas to something more closely resembling black and white, but without necessarily resorting to regulation or adjudication by the courts. See, for example, the discussion in its First Report on a Code of Conduct for Ministers to parallel the new Civil Service Code (1996) and the rules relating to the conduct of Members, HC 688 (1995–6).

[16] See note 1.

[17] Report of the Committee on Ministers' Powers, Cmd 4060 (1932).

[18] Report of the Committee on Tribunals and Inquiries, Cmnd 218 (1957).

[19] Erskine May, *Parliamentary Practice*.

[20] E.g., the Report of the Select Committee on *The Scrutiny of European Legislation*, HC 622, 1988–9, and the government's response, Cm 1081; 27th Report of the Select Committee on Procedure on *The Scrutiny of European Legislation*, HC 51, 1995–6.

[21] E.g., Fifth Report of the Select Committee on the Treasury and the Civil Service on *The Role of the Civil Service*, HC 27, 1993–4; the government's White Paper, *The Civil Service — Taking Forward Continuity and Change*, Cm 2748 (1994); Second Report of the Public Service Committee, *Ministerial Accountability and Responsibility*, HC 313, 1995–6, together with memoranda and minutes of evidence and First Special Report of the same committee, HC 67, 1996–7, which contained the government's response.

together the search does not stop short at the reports of official committees. Biographies and autobiographies may be a source, Harold Nicolson's of George V for example, as well as books by participating politicians,[22] which not only illustrate conventions at work but actually provide evidence of their existence and scope.

One result is that it is often difficult to get an overall picture of the constitution and of the relationship between the parts that a written constitution rooted in law provides. But if the British constitution is to be seen as a genuinely chosen alternative, it is arguable that it has to be seen as an equivalent to a written constitution. And if one wants to know what part the judges should play in it, it should be against the background of the constitution as a whole and not simply that part of it which for the time being falls within the jurisdiction of the courts. Indeed one could go further and argue that it should be seen against the background of constitutions and constitutionalism generally.

Judicial Review

And this applies in particular to judicial review. If it is to be given a truly constitutional foundation and a truly constitutional role some attempt must be made to see how it fits into the whole constitution, something which may be necessary even if the more limited aim of laying down general principles of judicial review is to be achieved. Two decades ago an attempt to integrate judicial review into the general constitutional structure would have seemed strange to many lawyers. It was difficult to see it even as a coherent unity in itself. In this it bore the marks of its origins as a largely do-it-yourself response of the courts to the growth of governmental power, itself a response to the new responsibilities taken on by governments in the face of increasing industrialisation and urbanisation in the nineteenth and twentieth centuries. Governments showed themselves far more ready to take new statutory powers than to provide remedies for those aggrieved by their exercise. The courts were left to do what they could with the materials available, the most innovative of which was the use of the ancient writ of certiorari which was basically a means by which the old court of King's Bench could review the activities of 'inferior courts', and then later, by adapting the remedy of declaration, which had long been available in the Court of Chancery in relation to private disputes, so that it could be used in disputes between citizen and government. On the basis of these remedies the courts slowly built up principles which were intended

---

[22] E.g., H. Wilson, *The Governance of Britain*; Lord Callaghan, *Time and Chance* (1987); Margaret Thatcher, *The Downing Street Years* (1993); N. Lawson, *The View from No. 11* (1992).

to prevent public bodies, in particular central and local government, exceeding the powers they had been given, limiting their use to the purpose for which they were given, and implying other refinements such as the duty to consider all relevant factors and ignore all irrelevant factors before reaching a decision or before taking action, whether or not any of these were spelled out in the statute granting the powers. The courts also showed a readiness to imply procedures for the exercise of statutory powers where none had been laid down by the statutes granting the power and even to supplement them where they had, insisting for example that what they called the rules of natural justice should be observed, e.g., that where property was being taken in the public interest the owner should be given at least an opportunity to make representations before a final decision was reached or action taken. There was also talk of a duty to act reasonably and a duty to act fairly.

But the development of a general system of administrative law and a general administrative jurisdiction was painfully slow. It was inhibited partly by the views of people like Dicey,[23] who had a tremendous influence on generations of lawyers and judges, that it was an essential and desirable feature of the British constitution that it did not have a specialist administrative jurisdiction like that in France, which in his view was bound to give preferential treatment to government, but that disputes between citizen and government should be dealt with by the ordinary courts in the ordinary way. In fact he claimed that this was one of the essential features of the rule of law which, along with the sovereignty of Parliament, he saw as the two major characteristics of the British constitution. And one can find these views echoed at various points in the subsequent history of dealing with the problems of the exercise of power by government, in the reports of the Ministers' Powers Committee for example, in 1932, and of the Franks Committee on Tribunals and Inquiries in 1957.

As was already mentioned in relation to the difficulty of developing general constitutional principles, another inhibiting factor was the piece-meal and fragmented nature of the relevant law. Decisions often turned not only on the wording of particular statutes but also on the peculiarities of the remedies the courts were using. As certiorari, for example, had been designed to review the activities of inferior courts, the courts felt it necessary to look for some judicial element in the exercise of the statutory power they were being asked to review. This was fine when it was a question of reviewing a decision of an administrative tribunal, more difficult when it came to looking at the activities of local authorities and

---

[23] A.V. Dicey, *The Law of the Constitution* (1884).

ministers of the central government. This led in turn to further problems when the courts, encouraged by the Ministers' Powers Committee, developed notions like quasi-judicial to enable them to get at functions which though basically administrative in nature could be said, at least at some stage, to have a judicial element. And the situation was not helped by some confusion between the requirement of a judicial element to enable certiorari to be used and the requirement of a judicial element to allow the courts to say that the principles of natural justice ought be observed. Many of the cases therefore turned on technicalities of this sort rather than basic merits. The details are not important. What is relevant though is that concern about whether or not the remedy was available often sidetracked the courts into technical arguments which were not really relevant either to the merits of the particular case or to the development of a general administrative jurisdiction based on general principles of administrative law, let alone a clear rationale of the basis of that jurisdiction in the context of the wider constitution.

Some of the progress was not only piecemeal, it was frankly accidental. In 1952 the Divisional Court in *Shaw*'s case[24] discovered that in the early nineteenth century certiorari had been used not only to review questions of procedure and excess of jurisdiction, but errors of law as well, and so gave the modern use of certiorari an unexpected fillip.

It was really only academic writers who saw in the hotchpotch of cases the basis of general principles. But even in their writings it was always noticeable how many of the generalisations were based on a particular series of statutes dealing with a particular area of government activity. Housing legislation dealing with slum clearance which was considered in such leading cases as *Arlidge* just before the First World War[25] and *Errington*[26] in the thirties loomed large just as cases under the Town and Country Planning Act did after World War II. Hence the kind of shock when a case like the Stevenage case occurred in which the House of Lords decided that the principles of natural justice which the courts had required to be observed in famous slum clearance cases like *Errington* did not have to be observed by the minister when designating the site of a new town under the New Towns Act and justified their decision on the grounds that it was a different statute with different wording.[27] This seemed to undermine a general principle though it also undermined the attempt to build up general principles on too slender a base.

---

[24] *R v Northumberland Compensation Appeal Tribunal, ex parte Shaw* [1952] 1 KB 338.
[25] *Local Government Board v Arlidge* [1915] AC 120.
[26] *Errington v Minister of Health* [1935] 1 KB 249.
[27] *Franklin v Minister of Town and Country Planning* [1948] AC 87.

It was not until 1977 when changes were made in the procedures for obtaining judicial review that the possibility of a breakthrough came. Many of the changes that have occurred since 1977 were not planned; if anything they were planned against. When the Law Commission in 1969 proposed to the Lord Chancellor a review of the whole system of judicial review of the activities of public bodies the proposal was turned down. Instead it was asked merely to look into and make recommendations about the procedures by which judicial review could be obtained. This it did, and came up with useful recommendations.[28] Instead of individual procedures for each of the writs traditionally used to review the activities of central and local government and other public bodies, a single procedure was laid down. A requirement of leave was added. New opportunities were given to obtain discovery of documents. All of these proposals were implemented first by a change in Order 53 of the Rules of the Supreme Court and were subsequently confirmed by the Supreme Court Act 1981. For the future, too, cases were to be set down on a special Crown Office list and were to be dealt with by designated judges in much the same way as commercial cases were given their own separate list and designated judges from 1894 until a separate Commercial Court was established in 1971. But what was prima facie merely a procedural change has been used by the judges to give a new lease of life to judicial review. It was not long before the House of Lords decided that one result of the change was that in future the Queen's Bench Division should have a monopoly of judicial review cases.[29] And there was talk in the courts of Britain having a body of administrative law.

These developments have given a new impetus to the expansion of the scope of judicial review and of the categories of people who can apply for it. But the consolidation of the jurisdiction has also given rise to further questions, in particular whether it is possible to provide some more general rationale for the jurisdiction and to set it more clearly and fully within the general constitutional framework.

Taking Conventions Seriously

What then needs to be done if the work of the courts is to be put on a firm foundation against the background of the constitution as a whole? A first step is to take conventions more seriously.

The tradition of not looking at the constitution as a whole goes back at least as far as Dicey. It was he who argued that because conventions do not impose legal obligations and do not fall directly within the jurisdiction of

---

[28] Law Commission Report No. 73, Cmnd 6407 (1976).
[29] *O'Reilly* v *Mackman* [1983] 2 AC 237.

the courts they are of no concern to lawyers. Indeed this court-oriented approach is one which affected British legal education and legal scholarship as a whole because of their image of the English legal system as essentially a made-in-court-by-the-judges system and their image of the student as future private practitioner with only court-oriented concerns. One must of course be careful not to exaggerate the influence of legal education on anyone but it is very likely that those who are currently judges did not as students study the constitution as a whole, and, even if they did, it was almost certainly only the British constitution in isolation and not against the background of constitutions or constitutionalism generally.[30] And it is extremely unlikely that they were taught of its having functions or what those functions are let alone alternative ways of performing them. Even today many law students are resistant to taking seriously what they regard as the vagueness of the conventional parts of the constitution, and often breathe a sigh of relief when they can get back to the familiar cases and judgments of the courts. But this is a luxury we can probably no longer afford. If the unwritten constitution is to survive it has to be taken seriously as a whole and this includes its conventions as well as its law, since one of the basic questions facing it is the extent to which the existing mix of conventions and law can operate as a genuine alternative, a real equivalent, to what it is claimed can be achieved by a shift to a written constitution.

Dicey's confusion of the jurisdiction of the courts and relevance to lawyers was mistaken for other reasons as well. Behind his sharp distinction between law and convention lies a picture of them as contiguous areas, of the one stopping where the other begins so that in effect they divide the constitution between them. But the distinction between law and convention is not as simple as that. They are not like bordering territories. Not only do law and convention often overlap and intertwine, the line between them is often arbitrary and changing. To exclude conventions from consideration not only distorts the picture of the constitution as a whole. It also makes it much more difficult to make sense of what is left. And not only that. Some of the more basic of them such as the sovereignty of Parliament and the use of precedent, and even the role of the courts themselves, can be seen as either law or convention according to the perspective from which one looks at them. There are, it is true, some pure conventions. The grand conventions which underlie the transfer of power from the monarch to governments responsible to Parliament are a prime example. And the rules of Parliamentary procedure are another. The

---

[30] See, e.g., D.I. Keir and F.H. Lawson, *Cases in Constitutional Law*, 5th edn (1967). Contrast G. Wilson, *Cases and Materials on Constitutional and Administrative Law*, 1st edn (1966).

purity of the conventions dealing with the procedures of the House of Commons is, as was mentioned earlier, reinforced by an express provision of the Bill of Rights of 1689 which prohibits the courts from interfering with them. But in other cases law and convention overlap and complement one another. Judicial independence provides a clear example.

When discussing judicial independence the books will point to the way in which the Act of Settlement of 1701 replaced the vulnerability of judges to dismissal by the King at his pleasure by a formula which said they were to remain in office as long as they behaved themselves (*quamdiu se bene gesserint*) and were only to be removed by a procedure which involved the support of Parliament. But of course the independence of the judges extends far beyond its provisions and is far more a matter of convention than law. The Act, for example, says nothing about appointment or promotion, or about the government not sending letters of instruction, advice or guidance to the judges about a particular case or sentence, or about judges not taking any notice of them if they did. It is convention which imposes an obligation on governments not to attempt to interfere with the judges in the exercise of their functions and which imposes a duty on the judges to be independent (supported by the oath they swear on appointment) as one can see more clearly if one imagines not a situation in which a government is attempting to pressure an unwilling judiciary but one in which there is a risk of the judiciary willingly colluding with those attempts. It is a particularly important convention that judges are not appointed or promoted or kept back on political grounds, when the system of appointment and promotion is largely in the hands of the government of the day or its Lord Chancellor (itself an office hedged around by conventions) rather than an independent commission. And even the Act of Settlement itself is not a fundamental statute in the sense that it cannot be repealed by simple majority. It depends for its special character on convention treating it as basic. This is another way in which law and convention intertwine. In the absence of any means of making a law fundamental in the British constitution because of the vulnerability of all law to change by simple legislation it is only convention which can give any law a fundamental or constitutional character.

A Constitutional Role for the Courts

One of the ways of encouraging the courts to look at the constitution as a whole would be for them to do something which they have not as yet done and that is to recognise explicitly that they have a constitutional role to play. Up till now the fact that many of their decisions have constitutional implications has never been raised to the level of seeing them as having a defined constitutional role let alone anything resembling a constitutional jurisdiction. But it would greatly help the integration of particular functions like judicial review into the constitution as whole if they were seen by the judges themselves as part of a more general constitutional function, not in any expansionist spirit, but in a way that is conscious of the desirability of an underlying unity of the constitution as a whole, including both its legal and its conventional parts. In some respects the addition of a jurisdiction over human rights foreshadowed by the proposed incorporation of the European Convention together with the existing jurisdiction of judicial review might be seen as foundations for such a development. But these developments, especially the incorporation of the Convention, may work both ways. While adding to the courts explicit constitutional jurisdiction in a particular field the latter may also have an inhibiting effect since the courts will come under intense scrutiny for any sign of 'politicisation' and will probably be tempted themselves to emphasise the limited impact of their new jurisdiction. It would probably therefore be better to see the notion of the courts having a general constitutional role to play as something independent of these developments. It should be seen instead as part of a move towards the notion that the courts are more than the products of their particular history, a move away from a position of subordinate independence towards something more like a separation of powers in which they form the judicial arm of the state and as such share in the maintenance and development of the constitution alongside and as partners with government and Parliament, though in a more limited way.

This constitutional jurisdiction would not of course in practice be as comprehensive as that of a constitutional court established by a written constitution. The first step would in many ways resemble the kind of opportunity that was given to judicial review when it was released from the particulars in which is was bogged down before 1977 or, to go further back, the opportunity that was given to rethink English private law when the old writs, forms of action and fictions were abolished in the nineteenth century and it became possible for broader notions of contract and tort to emerge, but without going so far as to adopt the overarching Continental law concept of obligation. The notion of judicial review has already escaped from being merely the sum total of isolated opportunities which the court took in the past to monitor the activities of government and other public bodies and has become a function in its own right albeit one subject, because of the doctrine of the sovereignty of Parliament, to modification by particular statutes. It is a short step to saying that this newly accepted role of judicial review is simply a particular example of the wider constitutional role of the courts which is similarly vulnerable to but not dependent on statute and which is similarly more than the total of individual instances that come their way. One of the attractions of taking such a step is the opportunity it would provide to give the legal jurisdiction a coherence based on an overall view of the constitution. It would also contribute to an underlying unity between the legal and the conventional parts of the constitution. And it would not be quite as unprecedented as at first sight it might appear. It has a recent precedent in the acceptance by the courts of their new role as European Community courts which goes beyond their administration of detailed Community law.

An Independent Jurisdiction

Up till now the courts have been very tentative about claiming an independent jurisdiction even as the basis of the narrower field of judicial review, let alone the constitution as a whole, and have soft-pedalled the notion of inherent powers. They have relied instead on a combination of what might be called accidents of history, like the availability of certiorari and precedent, as in *Shaw*'s case, and on generalised notions of the intention of Parliament, the implication of provisions and procedures, and presumptions of statutory interpretation, all of which can be seen as devices to avoid the courts asserting an independent and controlling jurisdiction.

Implied provisions have been a device the courts have used in both private and public law, justifying the implications in private law by reference to the presumed intention of the parties and those in public law by reference to the presumed intention of Parliament. In both cases the device has often worn thin. In private law it has caused difficulties in situations in which the parties had clearly not foreseen what had happened and the courts have attempted to do their best to make contracts effective, relying on the general intention of the parties or of parties in general, rather than the particular intention of the parties in the particular case. There were noticeable problems in this respect with the doctrine of frustration. Similarly when courts have rested their conclusions on the intention of Parliament the intention again is often a generalised and assumed intention of Parliament rather than the intention of Parliament in the particular statute, something that is clear when the courts operate on the basis of statutory presumptions. Statutory presumptions are in effect a set of values which the courts regard as important and which they will presume a statute did not intend to weaken unless it expressly says so, such as delegating a taxing power, making a criminal offence retrospective, not requiring *mens rea*. Here again the fiction occasionally wears thin especially when they are doing their best to avoid what seems on the face of it to be a clear intention to exclude their jurisdiction.[31]

If there has been a hesitation about resting judicial review on an independent base it is time it was put aside along with the notion that the basis of the court's judicial review jurisdiction rests on its historical power to review inferior courts which was the first justification for the courts intervening by way of certiorari.

To assert that they have an independent role to play would not be a novelty. It has always been the essence of the notion of common law that it is law which, though vulnerable to modification and change by Parliament, and though limited in the range of novelties which it can introduce, is in itself an independent source of law. In fact there is a tradition which not only makes it an independent source of law but which makes it fundamental or constitutional law as well.

One can find both views expressed by Chief Justice Coke as long ago as the seventeenth century. It was Coke who told King James I in the *Case of Prohibitions* (12 Co Rep 63 (1607)) that what his predecessors had done in setting up the common law courts could not be reversed and what had once been given could not be taken away, that the prerogative of administering justice had been irrevocably delegated to them. James I complained that he thought that the law was founded on natural reason and that he had as much natural reason as any man. Coke told him that far from being the product of natural reason it was artificial and required a good deal of diligence to acquire. And in the *Case of Proclamations* (12 Co Rep 74 (1611)) he went still further and claimed that the common law was an all-embracing concept and covered even the King's special prerogative powers. These too were part of the law of the land and by implication subject to the jurisdiction of the courts if any question as to their existence, scope or application arose. This was in effect a claim that the common law was a kind of fundamental law. And the King does not seem to have demurred, as he allowed challenges to his prerogative powers to be dealt with by the courts, sure no doubt in the knowledge that he could dismiss any judge at will, something that might encourage them to decide in his favour, for this was a time when, though the courts might be exercising an independent jurisdiction, the judges were still vulnerable to arbitrary dismissal by the King. Recent decisions asserting the power of the courts to review decisions made by bodies created by prerogative or the exercise of prerogative powers move in the same direction.

And in 1839 Lord Denman said the same about the privileges of Parliament in the case of *Stockdale* v *Hansard* ((1839) 9 Ad & El 1), a case

---

[31] E.g., *Anisminic Ltd* v *Foreign Compensation Tribunal* [1969] 2 AC 147.

that never seems to have been given the attention it deserves. When the House of Commons claimed that it could determine the existence and scope of its powers and privileges, Lord Denman told it that its powers and privileges, and those of Parliament as a whole, were part of the common law and therefore for the courts to determine, though it should be added that Parliament did not accept this. The dispute had to be settled by legislation, the Parliamentary Papers Act 1841, to which the courts immediately submitted. And since then both the courts and Parliament have been careful to avoid raising the issue again.

It is this notion of the common law as an independent and even fundamental law which makes declarations like that of Lord Diplock in *O'Reilly* v *Mackman* significant when he says that Britain after all and contrary to all previous beliefs does have a public law, since it confirms the view of Coke that the common law is not only there to provide answers to disputes between private citizens but between citizens and government as well. It is not a claim that the common law is the exclusive source of public law. However fundamental common law may be seen to be it will always need to be supplemented, complemented and even modified and changed by legislation. The courts share responsibility for both constitutional law and convention with government and Parliament. At the same time, ever since the abolition of the Court of Star Chamber in 1640, they have been quick to assert at least a controlling jurisdiction over any potential rival in the judicial field, as their reaction to the emergence of tribunals, and especially so-called administrative tribunals, in the twentieth century, has shown. Typically they have used the writ of certiorari as the basis of their intervention, using it for the purpose for which it was originally intended, to assert the pre-eminence of the courts over all 'inferior' jurisdictions.

It has to be admitted that the move from the common law as the historical product of particular courts in the past, the so-called common law courts of King's Bench, Common Pleas and Exchequer, to a notion of the common law as an independent and continuing source of the jurisdiction, ideas and principles of all the courts and of judge-made law in general needs both a degree of imagination and some sleight of hand, even in the limited field of judicial review and even more so if it is to be seen as the legal foundation of the whole constitution. Yet in a historically based constitution like the British, when one is talking law rather than convention, this is probably as attractive a way of looking at the position as any other since it can draw on a long tradition which has given the idea of the common law considerable prestige as well as a time-immemorial quality that makes it possible to regard it, somewhat romantically perhaps, as the pre-constitutional source from which the unwritten constitution has sprung, rather like Rome and Romulus and Remus, and, more importantly, from which it can continue to be renewed and refreshed.

But it has to be common law with a difference. It is important that this common law should not be seen as something which is time-bound and rooted in the past, or at least only in principle and not in its details, so that the search for relevant common law does not become a historical search for precedents. And though one of its attractions is that it has a kind of immemorial quality about it, it would have to break free from the tradition that for anything to be said to be justified by the common law it must have been shown to have existed since time immemorial, which is a hangover from the declaratory theory of judge-made law. Like convention it cannot be simply backward looking but must be subject to continuing scrutiny and capable of new development, subject to precedent but not dependent on it. To use the notion of common law in this context is to use it as a conception, a philosophy, an idea, and not as a body of rules embedded in the past. It is for use in the same creative spirit that a constitutional text, especially an ageing one, is used to match the law to changing circumstances and values. It would rest on the intention of Parliament not in the sense that that intention provided its foundation and justification but in the sense that Parliament had tolerated it. Sovereignty of Parliament does not mean that everything has to be authorised by Parliament, as the concurrent existence of prerogative powers shows. It means that everything is vulnerable to change by Parliament. It is a key feature of the common law, and judge-made law in general, that it is not the creation of statute though it is subordinate to it. Law has two sources of legitimacy, Parliament and the judges. And of course if the notion of common law as fundamental law were accepted even the doctrine of the sovereignty of Parliament would be subject to the decision of the courts when it came to questions of its existence and scope, as a matter of law and not just as a matter of convention.

And if the courts had judged the matter right and adopted a principle or concept that matched the constitutional expectations and requirements of the day there would be a convention to support it and so go some way to protect it from legislative change, just as convention supports the principle that an opportunity should be given to a person affected by a decision or action to make representations, which has come to be regarded as both something that ought to be included in a statute giving the power to take an action or make a decision as well as supporting non-interference by the legislature with the implication of that requirement by the courts if it had not been expressly included.

And the judges' constitutional role would not be confined to law. In spite of what Dicey said they have a direct role to play as regards convention as well. The fact that the constitution is made, remade, monitored and enforced by the major participants on a continuing basis has always been obvious as regards the grand conventions, those which developed as part of the transfer of power from monarch to ministers, and those other parts of the constitution in which the courts have traditionally played no role, such as the proceedings of Parliament. In all these cases the responsibility falls mainly on the members of the government and the opposition, the Speaker and the Parliamentary Commissioners and Members of Parliament generally. What is perhaps less obvious is that the judges too are not only custodians, interpreters and administrators of the law, operating within the traditional constraints of statute and precedent, but they also make up part of that amorphous body which watches over conventions as well, including not only those relating to the day-to-day administration of justice but also those relating to their own role in the wider constitution and their relationship with other parts of it, in particular government and Parliament. This is clear in relation to judicial independence. It is clear too that activities like judicial review are part and parcel of the general convention of the Rule of Law which speaks of the desirability of government by limited powers and fair procedures. But it goes even beyond that. The doctrine of the sovereignty of Parliament which has so dominated judicial thinking, the ways in which judges interpret and apply statutes, and the doctrine of precedent, are all rooted in convention whether or not they are seen as questions of law as well. They are traditions seen as binding, practices which continue to be accepted because of their constitutional appropriateness and desirability.

And just as in other cases it is possible for the major participants to review and revise old conventions and even create new ones, so it is the responsibility and even the duty of the judges to do so as well. And they have in fact done so. In 1966, for example, the House of Lords took what had hitherto been regarded as a fundamental feature of the legal system and unilaterally changed it. They made a judicial statement in which they said they would modify their traditional adherence to their own precedents, presumably in the belief that this was an area of activity which they had the right and responsibility to manage.[32] The gradual move away from a strictly literal to a more functional interpretation of statutes, and the U-turn in expressing a willingness to look at reports of the debates in Parliament to assist them are further examples.[33] Even more striking was the already mentioned departure from the orthodox doctrine of the sovereignty of Parliament when the House of Lords held that they would suspend the enforcement of a statute alleged to be in conflict with

---

[32] *Practice Statement (Judicial Precedent)* [1966] 1 WLR 1234.
[33] *Pepper* v *Hart* [1993] AC 593.

Community law, something which, as well as highlighting the dependence of that doctrine on its acceptance by the courts, showed another basic shift, with Lord Bridge saying no more in justification than it was the self-evident result of Britain's entry into the European Community.[34] And of course the readiness of the courts in response to the procedural changes made in the field of judicial review to lay the foundations of a recognisable jurisdiction and general principles of administrative law is itself a further recent example.

It goes almost without saying that in fulfilling their constitutional functions in this respect the judges need to have a picture of the constitution which goes beyond the strictly legal part and which shows it as a whole and which includes notions about their role and powers and the role and powers of the other major players in it, and which takes into account conventions as well as law.

The Doctrine of the Sovereignty of Parliament

One of the things that may have inhibited judges from seeing themselves as having a constitutional role is their acceptance of the doctrine of the sovereignty of Parliament. Not only have they accepted it in its narrow doctrinal sense, already wide enough, that there are no limits to what can be enacted by statute and that the courts will not question the validity of a statute on the grounds of its contents, they have allowed a more general notion of Parliamentary sovereignty to dominate their thinking about their general position in the constitution which has led them to show a more general deference to Parliament as the elected representative of the people. One of the questions that arises is whether this vulnerability to statute and this general deference should prevent the courts either taking conventions seriously or seeing themselves as having a genuine constitutional role to play alongside and not simply in a subordinate position to government and Parliament.

It should be said straight away that even the hard-core notion of the unlimited powers of statute is not as unassailable and self-evident as is usually suggested. Quite apart from the fact that, as a doctrine which is rooted in convention as well as law, its continuation in any form depends on its acceptance by the courts, its legal credentials also merit a closer look. The doctrine is clearly established in a number of particular instances where the courts have held, for example, that they would not be swayed by an argument that a statute violates generally accepted principles of international law or a treaty (other than the Treaty of Rome),

---

[34] See note 8.

even the European Convention of Human Rights, that it was no objection to the validity of a statute that it was retrospective even to the point of robbing a plaintiff of the benefit of a judgment of the House of Lords in its favour or that it was in breach of what would be regarded as a fundamental statute, e.g., Magna Carta or the Act of Union with Scotland. But it is a strange feature of writing on this subject that the strongest statements of the principle in all its glory, cited without comment in all the books, are from three cases on private railway Acts, in two of which the House of Lords said it was not prepared to listen to challenges to the validity of a statute on the grounds that the procedures of Parliament had not been observed in their enactment, something for which it did not need to rely on constitutional principle as this is something it had been told not to do by the Bill of Rights, together with a case in the Court of Queen's Bench in which the plaintiffs were told that they could not argue that a statute was invalid on the ground that it had been obtained from Parliament by fraud on the part of the promoters.[35] Somewhat surprisingly these three cases, all of which, besides being relatively trivial, centred on alleged failures of procedure and not the contents of the legislation, are constantly cited for the much wider proposition that the courts will not listen to any challenge to the validity of an Act of Parliament on any ground whatever. They are set alongside statements like that of Leslie Stephen, cited by Dicey, that if an Act of Parliament provided that all blue-eyed babies should be murdered that would be the law of the land which the judges would be under a constitutional duty to enforce.[36]

It is clear that none of these cases raised any real issue as to what the courts would and should do were they faced with legislation which clearly violated a basic constitutional or moral principle. A better test would be if the government and Parliament ever enacted a statute which was so abhorrent that the courts were forced to face up to this problem — imprisoning members of the opposition for example, or authorising the execution of a minority group. Everyone recognises that it is easier to have an absolute negative to intervention rather than run the risk of allowing a line to be drawn somewhere, which could vary with individual judges. At the same time there seems to be a real difficulty in saying on the one hand that to imagine such a statute being enacted is unthinkable without also saying that were such a statute enacted it is not unthinkable that the courts should be expected as a matter of law to enforce it. It may even be that the experience of Nazi Germany has modified views as to what is appropriate

---

[35] *Edinburgh and Dalkeith Railway* v *Wauchope* (1842) 8 Cl & F 710; *Lee* v *Bude and Torrington Junction Railway Co.* (1871) LR 6 CP 576; *British Railways Board* v *Pickin* [1974] AC 765.

[36] Dicey, op. cit., p. 81 citing Leslie Stephen, *Science of Ethics* (1882), p. 143.

and that today's judges, and if not today's then tomorrow's, ought to accept that experience of this kind can lead them to take a different view from that of judges dealing with cases involving private railway Acts in the nineteenth century and that it is not too late at the end of the twentieth to rethink the position.

Just as it can still be argued that the Queen has a reserve power to save the constitution by refusing to agree to legislation or by dismissing a government, even though in practice it might not prove effective, so too one can argue that the judges have a power of last resort to defend the constitution, and not simply by resigning. Nobody should be surprised if in a real case of legislative enormity the courts did not discover a higher principle of law by which they felt free or even obliged to ignore the current version of the doctrine not only in the name of constitutional convention but also in the name of law.

This suggests that even as a matter of strict law the doctrine is not as absolute and inviolable as it is usually presented. The fact that it is the courts which have the last word and may not yet have pronounced it, has been recently confirmed by their recent action in accepting the supremacy of Community law even over statute, something which shows that the doctrine is not as durable as was once thought and also that it ultimately depends on its continued acceptance by the courts.

The Rule of Law

But quite apart from doubts as to the real force and scope of the doctrine as a matter of law, the doctrine of Parliamentary sovereignty, especially in its fullest form, far from weakening the case for taking conventions seriously, actually strengthens it. It is the very strength of the traditional version of it that makes the convention summed up in the principle of the Rule of Law and indeed conventions generally so important. It is one of the functions of conventions that they can not only strengthen a law by giving it a fundamental character but they can also modify or limit the strict law. In Dicey's hands the principle of the Rule of Law included such things as the absence of a specialist administrative law jurisdiction such as existed in France at the time he was writing and the absence of a written guarantee of rights. But it is the third meaning he gave it that gives it its real force today, that government should not have arbitrary power, or, in its modern version, government should be carried on by means of limited powers, with its corollary that any excess should be challengeable in the courts. The Rule of Law is not in fact a rule of law. It is a conventional obligation which lies in the first instance on government and the legislature, since it is up to them what powers they bestow in the statutes which give public bodies their powers in the first place. In 1929, for example, the Committee on Ministers' Powers was set up in response to the publication by Lord Chief Justice Hewart of his book *The New Despotism*. One of the complaints he made was that Parliament was giving, and governments were taking, too many powers to make law themselves by means of delegated legislation and as a result undermining Parliament's position in the constitution as guardian of the law-making power, something on which historically, alongside the taxing power, its very place in the constitution had depended. In its report in 1932 the Committee argued that delegated legislative powers should be clearly defined, should not be wider than strictly necessary, that delegated legislation should be published, that the jurisdiction of the courts to determine whether the powers granted had been exceeded should not be excluded and that Parliament should set up a committee to examine the use made of delegated legislative powers. All these were in effect recommendations of new conventions which the Committee was arguing governments should accept. And the same is true of many of the recommendations of the Franks Committee on Tribunals and Inquiries, e.g., when it said that so-called administrative tribunals should be seen as part of the system of adjudication rather than of the administration and should be treated as bodies separated from the work of the departments whose decisions they are reviewing, and of the Committee on Immigration Appeals when it said that appeals against the decisions of officials are desirable as a matter of principle.[37] They are all recommendations for new conventions addressed to governments and Parliament in the first instance. And though governments and Parliament may fail to implement them in a particular case this would not destroy their validity as conventions if those principles came to be accepted as fundamental parts of the constitution.

Even the developing area of judicial review rests in the last resort on convention. All of its principles and remedies, in fact judicial review as a whole, are as a matter of law vulnerable to modification or even removable by statute. But it is an important aspect of the Rule of Law that this jurisdiction should be preserved and that the standards on which courts are insisting should be observed.

It follows that the doctrine of the sovereignty of Parliament far from weakening the case for taking conventions seriously and looking at the constitution as a whole strengthens it since it is clear that without such conventions as the Rule of Law some of the main aims of having a constitution at all would not be achieved. It is, too, because of the doctrine of the sovereignty of Parliament, which enables any law to be changed by

---

[37] Committee on Immigration Appeals, Cmnd 3387 (1967).

simple statute, that it is only convention which gives even the relevant legal rules their constitutional or fundamental character. From a legal point of view all law is equally changeable. There does not seem to be a method of 'entrenching' a particular statute or protecting it by requiring a special majority for its amendment or repeal and the same applies to basic court decisions in the constitutional field. It is only convention which protects even basic laws from unconstitutional change, just as it is only convention which prevents governments abusing their majority powers.

And this is one of the points at which one is faced with a conscious choice. Are convention and self-regulation enough? Do they offer safeguards equivalent to those offered by a constitution rooted in law, laid down in a written text and supported by a constitutional court, or do they have any other advantages which compensate for any weaknesses they may have in this respect?

Before coming to that, however, in thinking about the constitutional role of the courts there is a second aspect of the court's attitude to Parliament that needs to be considered, not the one which springs from their acceptance of the doctrine of the sovereignty of Parliament in its narrower sense, but the one which puts the courts more generally in a subordinate position to Parliament, on the ground of the latter's special position in the constitution as the elected representative of the people. How far should this affect the courts' picture of their position and role in the constitution?

It could of course be argued that this attitude exaggerates the representative character of the Queen-in-Parliament as a whole, the combination of the House of Commons, House of Lords and the Queen whose agreement is needed for the enactment of a statute, although the powers of the House of Lords are restricted both by convention and the Parliament Acts of 1911 and 1949 and the Queen's assent is assumed — it has not been refused since 1707, though George V thought about doing so in 1914 but in the end decided it would serve no useful purpose.[38] A refusal suffers from the serious defect that any crisis grave enough to justify a refusal would be likely to be unaffected by it; in addition to it probably resembling a bee sting — its use would result in the departure of the bee.

Even in relation to the House of Commons itself it could also be argued that in so far as it was the extension of the franchise that led the courts to show a greater deference to Parliament, this may have been both premature and misguided, though understandable in an age which attached so much importance to the extension of the vote.

---

[38] Harold Nicolson, *George V* (1952), p. 234.

The fact is that seen against the background of the constitution as a whole, the notion of the sovereignty of Parliament and the continued use of the notion of the Queen-in-Parliament is misleading. Talk of the Queen-in-Parliament in relation to legislation obscures the fact that it is not the Queen-in-Parliament that enacts legislation but the government-in-Parliament, in a combination in which the government not only has a dominant political role but has and is intended to have a dominant constitutional role as well. Similarly the continued expressions of a general deference to the sovereignty of Parliament obscure the fact that the deference is being paid not to Parliament but, both as a matter of political fact and constitutional principle, to the government-in-Parliament. And this is not the only factor that clouds the true position. The constant emphasis by the courts on that aspect of the doctrine of the sovereignty of Parliament which speaks of unlimited powers diverts attention from another equally important aspect of the doctrine, which is nearer to its historical origins, that it is intended to impose limitations on government. This is the aspect which emphasises that there are limits to what governments can do on their own and that they can only do certain things in certain ways, one of which is that they must obtain Parliamentary approval in the ways laid down by the formal procedures of Parliament. Historically the leading examples of these things were making and changing the law and imposing taxation and the doctrine was an important step in securing Parliament's position and role in the constitution vis-à-vis the king and his ministers, one of the triumphs in fact of the defeat of the Stuart kings in the seventeenth century. Here the emphasis is not on unlimited powers. It is the reverse. It does not emphasise the subordination of the courts but is intended to be a brake and a check on government. Together with the wider conventional principle of ministerial accountability (or responsibility) to Parliament it remains one of the main buttresses of the role of Parliament as a central forum of debate and of the Parliamentary procedures which guarantee the opposition its opportunities to criticise and present itself as an alternative government. It is therefore one of the foundations of the Parliamentary system of government. It is the reason why an Enabling Act of the kind which Hitler extracted from the Reichstag or of the kind that Sir Oswald Mosley proposed for the United Kingdom in 1931[39] would strike a blow at the heart of the constitution. It is also the reason why the Committee on Ministers' Powers recommended caution and safeguards as regards the practice of delegating to government powers to legislate.

---

[39] See his evidence to the Select Committee on Procedure, HC 161, 1931–2.

But though the obligation on the government to use the Parliamentary process and to account to Parliament for its activities and policies was intended to act as a check it has come to be accepted that it is not intended to be an absolute check. Convention and the rules of Parliamentary procedure themselves guarantee that, after due debate, the government will, on the whole, get its way. That this is not just a question of political fact but is built into the constitutional structure is shown by the fact that a government is only entitled to be a government as long as it can command a majority in the House of Commons. Parliament is not intended to be an independent agent whose consent has to be won in the way in which the President of the United States has to win the support of Congress for legislation, for example. A principle which once was the foundation of Parliament's position vis-à-vis the government is now the foundation of the opposition's right against the government-in-Parliament.

For the courts to narrow their conception of their role on the basis of the increasingly representative character of the House of Commons as a result of the gradual extension of the franchise misses the point that, just at the time when the franchise was being extended, not only were the powers and responsibilities of government increasing, but the independence of Parliament was decreasing and, not just as a matter of political practice, but as part of an accepted constitutional development. It might have been possible in the middle of the nineteenth century to speak of Parliament as independent and having an independent role to play. But the rise of the political and constitutional importance of political parties put an end to that.

Political parties are an example of the overlap between political practice and constitutional convention. At one extreme political parties look like private interest groups outside of the constitution, using it for their own advantage. At the other it seems clear that important parts of the current constitutional arrangements not only assume their existence but depend on them for their effective operation. In fact the current constitutional conventions go even further. Not only do they support the existence of political parties, they support the existence of large political parties. The convention of the collective responsibility of the government to Parliament reflects this. The present arrangements assume a government formed by a disciplined political party, something reflected in the cases on Parliamentary privilege which distinguish pressure on Members of Parliament put on them by their party whips from pressures put on them by outside bodies. Governments are not only expected to present a united policy, and not leave large numbers of issues to a free vote, but also to present a single target, subject in principle to being defeated as a whole and not a many headed Hydra which produces a new head as soon as an old one has been lopped off, so that they stand or fall together and cannot simply re-form in case of defeat. This is what is meant by collective responsibility. And here again one sees the mix of political practice and constitutional convention. What is from one point of view the imposition of party discipline in its own interests is also a principle of constitutional importance.

Everyone knows that this may in some cases end up in the collective defence of the indefensible — including the indefensible individual minister — and that it discourages public dissent among what is now the large number of Members of Parliament holding ministerial posts. But that is the current convention. The existence of strong disciplined parties is not only reflected in expectations of the government but also of the opposition which is intended to be in a position to act as an alternative government as well to act as a monitor and critic of government policy and administration. The notion of having political parties which can form effective governments and effective alternative governments lies, too, behind the current preference for a first-past-the-post system of election which is defended as encouraging the continuance of large parties rather than a multiplicity of smaller parties.

Looking at the reality of the constitutional situation in this way may not be seen as a sufficient ground for challenging the doctrine of the sovereignty of Parliament head on but it is important that general constitutional attitudes underlying the activities of the courts should be rooted not only in reality but in principles which reflect the constitutional reality and the danger avoided that misleading language may lead to misled results. So far as judicial review is concerned this means that, instead of making such a sharp distinction between government and Parliament, and allowing themselves to pay formal deference to the latter when they are paying factual deference to the former, the courts should see Parliament for what it is, a body dominated by government. It might even be right to go further and to see statutory powers for what they are, powers which the government was required to obtain in a particular way but that in acquiring them the government has not obtained the endorsement of an independent Parliament. It has had simply to go through particular processes which are in themselves regarded as valuable, but which do not amount to an independent, or provide the possibility of an absolute, check.

Characteristics of Conventions

Taking both conventions and law into account does not of course mean one should ignore the differences between them as this is something which has

to be taken into account when weighing the pros and cons of convention/
self-regulation as against the use of law.

Conventions will often not have the rigour of legal rules. It is in their
nature that there will often be areas of uncertainty and about when 'has in
the past' becomes 'ought in the future' or whether 'ought' in the past has
now lost its persuasive or binding character because of changing views or
circumstances. Of course there is always scope for more conventions to be
set out in a more detailed and codified form, and even for provision to be
made for determining their scope and application[40] without going the
whole hog and moving to a written constitution or even involving law and
the courts. But where they have not been translated into law or take the
form of rules of one kind or another and where no special procedure has
been adopted for their definition, interpretation and enforcement, they will
often be open-ended and subject to debate. Has the use of a Speaker's
Conference, for example, become a conventional requirement for major
changes in the electoral system? How should the House of Commons
handle the reports of the Boundary Commissioners?

And just as it may sometimes be difficult to draw a clear line between
political practice and constitutional convention so it may sometimes be
difficult to distinguish constitutional debate about their existence and
scope and whether they have been broken from party political debate. This
is something to which Lord Nolan refers in discussing the way in which
the doctrine of the individual responsibility of ministers may work in
practice, especially when it comes to the question of whether a particular
minister should or should not resign, though this kind of overlap is
paralleled in countries with written constitutions where a legal constitutional challenge can be mounted as a political tactic.

Not only can there be uncertainty about the scope and applicability of
conventions in a particular case but there may also be problems about their
enforcement. It is another major feature of conventions that they often
depend on a form of self and mutual regulation. Governments are expected
to observe the constitutional limits of their powers not, for example, to use
their majorities to legislate in an arbitrary or despotic way or to change the
rules of Parliamentary procedure to their advantage. The opposition is
expected to oppose in a responsible manner and not engage in a deliberate

---

[40] As is the case with the proceedings and privileges of the House of Commons where the
Speaker is authorised to make rulings and the Select Committee on Privileges and
Standards can consider allegations of breaches of privilege and contempt. Allegations
of maladministration can be referred to the Parliamentary Commissioner for Administration and alleged breaches of the codes of conduct to the Parliamentary Commissioner
for Standards.

policy of obstruction of the kind engaged in by Parnell and the Irish Nationalists in the 1880s which was designed to bring the business of Parliament and the government to a halt.

As there is no constitutional court to which an appeal can be made if it is alleged that governments have behaved unconstitutionally, observance is often a matter of self-regulation, with pressure coming from criticism from the opposition, in the media, adverse public opinion and finally through the ballot box. However, far from being seen as a weakness the reliance on self and mutual regulation is often claimed as one of the virtues of the British system because it places responsibility where in reality it lies in all constitutions, on the major actors.

All constitutions depend on the willingness of those engaged in governmental activities to observe not only the letter of the law but the spirit of constitutionalism that underlies it. The experience of written constitutions which have failed even when their letter has been observed, as happened in the case of the Weimar Republic, let alone of those which have failed where it has not, clearly support this view. Leaving it to a constitutional court and the letter of the law, it is also said, may reduce the willingness of governments and others to observe the rules in the first place much in the same way as Sir Stephen Sedley cites the practice of macho-administrators who leave what should have been checked at an earlier stage for the courts to control by means of judicial review.

Rethinking the Role of the Past

In the absence of a written constitution the British constitution is bound to rely on the past not only to cover the ground which would otherwise be covered by the written text but also to provide the legitimacy which a written constitution would otherwise provide. And this applies particularly to the judges, who rely on the past, and particularly the past in the form of precedent, as one of the main justifications for what they do independently of statute. But reliance should not mean absolute dependence.

Conventions, for example, are not binding simply because they reflect past practice but also because that past practice continues to reflect current constitutional expectations and values. The precedents are not binding in the way that precedents are binding in the British courts. So the King's secretary, Lord Stamfordham wrote in June 1929, 'the fact is that you and I, who naturally are inclined to look back to precedents, must remember that they are almost as little applicable to England today as they would be to China'.[41] When George VI was called upon in 1940 to decide whether to invite Lord Halifax or Churchill to form a government he could look back on the precedent of his father George V, who had to choose between Curzon and Baldwin in 1923. But, leaving aside political factors, what was constitutionally important was not the past precedents but the underlying rationale of having the prime minister in the House of Commons which had become a constitutional expectation in a way that it apparently was not when Queen Victoria invited Lord Salisbury to form a government in 1895.

This emphasis on a modern rationale for conventions is important in another respect as well. When people look back over the years during which the British constitution developed without much forethought, the virtues of lack of forethought, like lack of principle, may be exaggerated. It is true that in years past the constitution has often developed in this way. But times have changed. This is one of the major differences between the treatment of conventions in the past and the treatment of conventions at the present time. We have gone past the stage when, as Dicey put it, the constitution could be seen as 'the fruit of that instinct which . . . has enabled Englishmen . . . to build up sound and lasting institutions, much as bees construct honeycombs, without undergoing the degradation of understanding the principles on which they raise a fabric more subtly wrought than any work of conscious art'.[42] The reliance on convention is no longer merely a historical accident. It is now a choice between alternative means, an alternative to a written constitution rooted in law, a preferred tool of constitutional development and a preferred means of achieving constitutional propriety. As Lord Nolan's Committee shows, it is both possible and necessary from time to time to create new conventions. The standards and procedures Lord Nolan's Committee has recommended are not simply sharpening the means of implementing old values, they are also making a knowing and positive contribution to the creation of new conventions, recommending new standards reflecting new values, with new institutions and procedures to give effect to them. And once established they will be more than policy changes. They will create institutions which in their own way will become as much part of the conventional constitution as the grand constitutional conventional institutions of prime minister and cabinet.

---

[41] Harold Nicolson, *George V* (1952), p. 434. The way in which the closure and guillotine procedures have become part of the normal Parliamentary process is a good example of the importance of the constitutional rationale in the acceptance of a convention. For here was a practice introduced for one purpose, to prevent deliberate obstruction of the proceedings of the House of Commons, being used for another, setting a time limit to ordinary debate, because it fitted in with what was seen as the appropriate balance of power between government and opposition in the conduct of business in the House.

[42] Dicey, op. cit., p. 3.

It is one of the marked differences between countries with a written constitution and Britain that in the former the constituent assembly meets, drafts and adopts a written constitution and departs. From the day the constitution is adopted its work is done. It is the written text and the institutions provided for in the constitution, together with any provisions for amendment, that take over. In the British situation the constituent assembly never meets on a single occasion to adopt a single constitutional framework or set of principles. It is, in effect, constantly in session, constantly in a position to adapt the old and create something new and it does not have to do so within the framework of a written text or by way of a complicated amendment procedure. It can be experimental, tentative and pragmatic. And although one should not ignore the stimulus to creativity that having to develop principles from a text provides, just as working from a text of a code often does in private law, its creativity covers a wider range than a constitutional court which, while it may be very good at developing new and adapting old principles, cannot, for example, create new institutions or new procedures or modify old ones with the same freedom.

And what is true of conventions is true of the constitution as a whole. While an unwritten constitution like the British has to rely heavily on the past this reliance too must be a question of conscious choice so that, in using the heritage of the past, it does not fail to meet the demands and expectations of the present and future. From this point of view some parts of the constitution not only have a distinctly old-fashioned look, especially when compared with other constitutions. They also raise some serious questions about the continued suitability of some of the key concepts inherited from the past. The continued use of notions such as the Queen-in-Parliament and even the sovereignty of Parliament have already been mentioned. Two further examples are the continued use of the notions of Crown and prerogative to describe the government and its inherent and residual powers.

It is one of the weaknesses of not having a picture of the constitution as a whole, that the judges have not found it possible to think in general terms about the executive, legislature and the judiciary, and executive, legislative and judicial powers, in the manner of the United States constitution. Instead they have spoken much more about the Crown (not even the government), ministers (with Secretaries of State forming a special category), Parliament and the courts. And instead of feeling free to attribute to them the general powers appropriate to their functions in the constitution they have instead felt obliged to determine the existence and scope of their (non-statutory) powers by reference to precedent. It is as if, whereas in the field of convention the transition from monarchy to

Parliamentary government has not only been acknowledged but accepted, epitomised early on in Bagehot's contrast between the dignified and the efficient parts of the constitution, with the monarchy belonging to the former rather than the latter, the legal part of the constitution is still caught in the time warp of the seventeenth century. Whereas in the field of convention the use of the descriptions, Her Majesty's government and Her Majesty's opposition and the Queen's speech, are seen for what they are, gentle reminders of a past tradition with no further impact, the notions of Crown and prerogative still play a part in legal reasoning and may play a decisive part in the outcome of particular cases.[43]

The notion of prerogative has a long history. At some point in time it came to be used to describe and explain the special inherent or traditional powers of the King. It was particularly pressed into service in the seventeenth century when the powers of the King to act independently of Parliament were being challenged. It is then we hear of the prerogative power to regulate the import and export of goods, to imprison, to act in the defence of the realm. The notion of the Crown seems to have been the way in which the law attempted to cope with the transition from the personal rule of the King to rule by ministers and governments in his name. Since then the government, disguised as the Crown, has been said to have inherited most of the prerogative powers of the King. What might have happened was that the prerogative might have been identified with the inherent, necessary and residual powers of government and so provided an old name for a new concept. But that is not what happened. Instead, as part of a general scaling down of the prerogative power at a time when it was seen as something to be limited, constrained or even extinguished, it has increasingly come to be spoken of in terms of a bundle of individual prerogative powers, limited in number and limited in scope, and issues about the scope of the non-statutory powers of the government have been dealt with by a search for precedents to show a particular prerogative power existed.

In the *Burmah Oil* case in 1964,[44] for example, where the company was claiming compensation for its oil installations which had been destroyed by British armed forces to prevent them falling into the hands of the Japanese armed forces in Burma in 1942, the discussion was not about the inherent powers of modern governments in time of war or other emergency. The decision was made to turn on writings of seventeenth and eighteenth-century constitutional writers (as the case was begun in Scotland) and cases like the *Case of Saltpetre* in 1607 (12 Co Rep 12). Of course everyone recognised that it would have been better if the matter had

---

[43] E.g., *Town Investments Ltd* v *Department of the Environment* [1978] AC 359.
[44] *Burmah Oil Co. Ltd* v *Lord Advocate* [1965] AC 75.

been regulated by statute from the beginning, as it eventually was after the House of Lords reached its decision. But given that it was not, anyone looking at the case is bound to conclude that it has an antiquarian, even an archaeological, quality about it. It can also give the impression that important constitutional matters are being decided by historical accident, or at least by reference to precedents from very different times and circumstances.

And the notion of government as Crown has not done much better. Here too instead of using the Crown as an old-fashioned way of describing government, conclusions have been drawn from the fact that the government was now exercising the powers of the Crown, rather than acting as the government of a modern state. It was not so long ago that when constitutional law books came to talk about the civil service they were preoccupied with cases in which attempts to establish some kind of employment relationship between civil servants and the government were frustrated by the notion that all civil servants, commissionaires and lift attendants at ministry offices in London included, were servants of the Crown and that the Crown's power to dismiss them at will could not be fettered because of the risks that might otherwise result on the frontiers of the old colonial empire, if a sun-kissed local administrator mismanaged a local crisis.[45] And the courts themselves have also got caught up in this old-fashioned way of looking at things. In 1947 the Crown Proceedings Act had to come to the rescue to enable actions to be brought against the government because an action against the government was seen as an action against the Crown and therefore in some way impossible to maintain in the 'King's' courts.

Not only has the use of these notions proved inhibiting, it has also proved inadequate and has resulted in uncertainty. The government's power to contract, for example, can probably best be seen as the result of the government having the same powers and capacities as any other corporation or fictitious entity, so that it has the power to contract just like a run-of-the-mill company does. But then one suddenly finds the courts saying that government contracts have characteristics which other con-tracts do not have, the usual hallmark of a prerogative power, so that, for example, governments cannot be held to have contracted in such a way as would fetter their future executive action.[46] And there are other cases in which, in despair, prerogative has been used as a last resort to justify a power which it is acknowledged exists but for which no other authority can be found. The Privy Councillors appointed to look into the

---

[45] E.g., *Dunn* v *The Queen* [1896] 1 QB 116; *Dudfield* v *Ministry of Works, The Times,* 24 January 1964.

[46] *Rederiaktiebolaget Amphitrite* v *The King* [1921] 3 KB 500.

government's powers to tap telephones turned to prerogative in this way in the absence of any other authority for it.[47]

All these considerations expose weaknesses in the use of both Crown and prerogative as basic concepts of constitutional and administrative law, of trying to treat the powers of modern government on the basis of a historical approach to a historical concept and raise questions as to whether it continues to make sense to see government as some kind of generalised or transformed King, as the transfer from the concept of King to the concept of the Crown tries to do. It is arguable that the powers and role of government need a more up-to-date explanation, justification and rationale. The notions of Crown and prerogative are probably too deeply rooted in the strict law and precedent to be removed or modified by the courts alone, and the help of government and statute may be needed, as has now happened in relation to telephone tapping and as happened with proceedings against the government after the courts eventually refused to carry on with the fiction they had introduced in an attempt to alleviate the situation. But to whatever extent it may still be necessary as a result of the force of binding precedent to use the notions it seems pretty clear that they should be downgraded from their status as basic or orientating concepts to more or less unsatisfactory instrumental concepts and not regarded as foundation principles of constitutional law from which general principles and detailed rules can be developed. And just as the progress of administrative law should not depend on the kind of historical exposition which gave a new lease of life to certiorari in *Shaw*'s case so the future of the British constitution should not depend on the kind of lottery analysis of the past which fills the pages of the House of Lords judgment in the case of *Burmah Oil*.

Rethinking the Past

But rethinking the past goes beyond rethinking particular concepts which have become embedded in rules of law. As was mentioned earlier the past plays a more general role in an unwritten constitution. It provides part of the foundations, explanation and justification for the ways in which the major participants go about their tasks and indeed what those tasks are. In addition to supplementing the past with conceptions more directly relevant to the present there may be both scope and need for a revision of current conceptions of the past itself. This is not a review in the light of new historical research, for the courts do not operate on the basis of real history, the kind of history that is vulnerable to or determined by historical

---

[47] Statement of the findings of Privy Counsellors on the interception of communications, Cmnd 283 (1957).

research. They operate on the basis of an assumed, conventional, one might even say consensual, history in which historical events and institutions often have a symbolic value. It is, therefore, a review with a view to arriving at a new consensus, a new consensus which gives a picture of the past which not only gives a better understanding of the present but also better meets its needs and reflects its values.

In this history particular milestones are given the kind of status which is given to particular cases such as *Donoghue* v *Stevenson* ([1932] AC 562) in private law and the *Wednesbury Corporation* case[48] in public law. They become a kind of shorthand and reference point, something which needs no further justification, like the text of a code or constitution. The Court of Star Chamber, for example, stands in the present canon as a symbol of oppression and the danger of special courts for dealing with alleged offences against the state which no amount of historical research which presents it as a harmless small claims court will overturn. The fact that the court has not been replaced in people's minds by Hitler's Volksgerichtshof is both a tribute to its tenacity as symbol and the continuing insularity of British constitutional thought.

But the identification of particular milestones in this way, as Sir Stephen notes in relation to the *Wednesbury* case, may give them an importance they cannot or should not have or should no longer have, and may wrongly overshadow other equally important events that deserve more attention though for some reason they have not caught the imagination or been included in the received tradition.

When one looks at the current conventional history major landmarks or milestones clearly stand out in the language and rhetoric of the law; Magna Carta, the Stuart struggle, the Bill of Rights, the development of the office of prime minister and cabinet government. But there is a major gap which fundamentally distorts the picture as a whole and it is something that will need to be redressed if a better and more realistic picture of the general background to the present position is to be won. Current conceptions of constitutional development fail to do justice to the revolutionary changes which occurred in Britain in the nineteenth century and which have occurred in Britain and elsewhere since. Here the conventional catalogue is dominated by the Reform Act of 1832, which began the extension of the franchise and, not an event, but a person, Dicey, whose identification of the sovereignty of Parliament and the Rule of Law as major and desirable features of the constitution has dominated so much legal thinking about the British constitution ever since, and who survived major attacks by Professors Jennings and Robson as late as the 1930s.

---

[48] *Associated Provincial Picture Houses Ltd* v *Wednesbury Corporation* [1948] 1 KB 223.

Britain did not have the revolutions which shook France in 1830 and 1848 or anything like the *coup d'état* of Napoleon III or the defeat at the hands of Prussia in 1871, or the meetings of the Frankfurt Assembly in 1848 or the foundation of the Second Empire in Germany. Nor did its public law have anything resembling the clear revolutionary changes in the field of private law which resulted from the abolition of forms of action and the reconstruction of the courts in 1873–75. But the emphasis on the extension of the franchise and the views of Dicey fail to do justice to the revolutions that did in fact occur in nineteenth-century Britain which have affected the constitution in general and the role of the courts and especially judicial review in particular.

One reason for the fact that these events are still overshadowed in the language and rhetoric of the law may be that the major changes took place outside of the courts and, in so far as they were reflected in law, they were reflected more in legislation than judge-made law, the general impact of which a system based on precedent is often slow to absorb. In fact this is the age when legislation took over from judge-made law as the dominant form of law and laid the foundations of those developments to which the development of judicial review was a response. The vast increase in government responsibilities arising from the need to cope with the rise of factories, towns and railways, the concern for the way in which the poor law was administered, for public health and the environment and education, leading on to the foundation of the welfare state under the Liberal government which came to power in 1906, the transformation or, more accurately, the creation of central and local government, and of a politically neutral civil service, the emergence of relatively stable and disciplined major political parties led by identifiable leaders, organised on a nationwide basis, the cleansing of elections and their acceptance as the decisive factor as to who should form a government, the way in which governments came to dominate the business and the time of the House of Commons, the almost final withdrawal of the monarch from the political scene (delayed somewhat by Queen Victoria and not fully completed until the reign of George V in the present century) are simply some of the events that mark out the nineteenth century as a watershed to the point that it can almost be seen as a new beginning, even if there seems to have been a conspiracy to disguise it, as even the architecture of the House of Commons shows. It may even be the nineteenth century which placed the emphasis on the seventeenth century which it still has in basic legal constitutional thinking. It is a major weakness of the present rhetoric, the present language of British constitutional law, that no way seems to have been found to inject these developments into the current conventional legal history. None of these have been acknowledged as the foundations of the present system which in fact they are. And this is a particularly serious weakness when it comes to looking at the administrative jurisdiction of the courts which, as was said earlier, is one of the major responses of the courts to them.

There is another sense too in which the courts may need to review their attitudes to the past and its lessons before they can move confidently ahead. In any look back there is a need for the judges to come to grips with their own past. They need to reflect and engage with the past and come to terms with it. For it is a paradox that at the same time as the judges in the nineteenth century were making strong statements about the sovereignty of Parliament they were also having great difficulty in accepting at least some of its legislation at its face value. This was so obvious in the case of trade union legislation, which attempted first to make unions lawful associations and then to make lawful at least some of the actions they were likely to take in the course of industrial disputes, that, following the *Taff Vale* case in 1901[49] the Liberal government in 1906 enacted the Trade Disputes Act to remove them from the scene altogether. The failure of the courts to provide the simple means of settling disputes that the Workmen's Compensation Act of 1906 had envisaged and later the stigma attached to them as a result of the role of the National Industrial Relations Court under the Industrial Relations Act of 1971, as well as major confrontations with Parliament in the series of cases surrounding Stockdale in the late 1830s and Bradlaugh in the 1880s,[50] all these are major events which help shape current attitudes both of other people to the role of the judges and the judges' own views of their role which they will have to take into account when considering what their role in the future could and should be. Judges will have to accept that anything that looks as if they are asserting a more prominent role in the constitution will be met by arguments not only based on their present competences and character but also on incidents in the past which will need to be explained and where necessary explained away. Attempts have been made, as in *Duport Steels Ltd v Sirs* ([1980] 1 WLR 142) but the kind of statements made so far amount to little more than a warning to be heeded rather than the last word when it comes to looking at the role of the judges in the constitution at large.

The Future: a Summary

The first step is to see the constitution as a whole and as the real equivalent of deliberately constructed constitutions, intended to achieve similar goals to those intended to be achieved by a written constitution and a

---

[49] *Taff Vale Railway Co.* v *Amalgamated Society of Railway Servants* [1901] AC 426.
[50] *Bradlaugh* v *Clarke* (1883) 8 App Cas 354; *Bradlaugh* v *Gossett* (1884) 12 QBD 271.

constitutional court, with the use of convention being seen as an alternative to the use of law and not just a historical accident.

Second, for the courts to see themselves as constitutional courts with a limited jurisdiction, including judicial review. Although their role in this respect is not an overriding role or even a comprehensive role of the kind that is associated with constitutional courts it should be seen as a principled jurisdiction, not one just made up of bits and pieces but one rooted in a general constitutional philosophy. And it should include conventions as well as law.

Third, for the courts to emphasise that they have an independent role, albeit one which is subject to legislative intervention though the role of the courts and their particular contributions may be protected by constitutional convention even when they are not protected by law. There should in any event be some caution in accepting the widely held view that there are no legal limits to what can be enacted by legislation.

Fourth, reassess the role of the past history and precedent. Emphasise utility and consistency with current expectations as not only a test of continued adherence to precedent and traditional attitudes but as the basis of new developments. If concepts like the Crown and prerogative are to continue to be used it must be with a more generalised awareness of what it is they are intended to achieve rather than in a fatalistic way, as if the matter was already in some way implicitly resolved in the materials inherited from the past.

Fifth, infuse the particular notions of the Crown and government with generalised notions of the state and the executive. See the judges as the judiciary and as the third arm of the state.

Sixth, in looking at the past as a whole, in particular in the context of judicial review, give the nineteenth century more attention than the concepts of the seventeenth-century struggles. And in looking at the nineteenth century it is not just a question of looking out for currently undervalued or under-emphasised precedents, legal history in its narrowest sense, though there may well be scope for this, but of giving more weight and attention to the major changes outside of the law which were reflected in the new emphasis on government and administration and the statutory powers which were given to them to enable them to meet their new responsibilities. In the new conventional history it should not be so much King, Crown and prerogative that should loom large, but factories, towns and political parties, and not just British precedents but at least European, not ready acceptance of the doctrine of the sovereignty of Parliament without regard to the experience of the Nazi regime, not the Star Chamber but Hitler's Volksgerichtshof, not simply the Committee on Ministers' Powers and delegated legislation but Hitler's Enabling Act.

And so far as general principles are concerned generalise the principle of the rule of law to see it as the British equivalent of constitutionalism, and in particular the principle of government by limited powers.

Seventh, the fact that the major conventions and even judicial review developed at such a slow pace does not mean that this is the appropriate pace and method for an unwritten constitution. The lessons have been learnt. Convention is now an alternative to law and not simply a historical hangover and new conventions can be created. Judicial review is now a basic convention and its integration into the wider constitution can be far more rapid than its slow progress in the past.

And finally there is no need to wait for what might be seen at first sight as a programme for legal scholarship and legal education to work its way through the system. It could be a programme for lawyers and judges in the more immediate future. It is not too much to hope that the Judicial Studies Board should play its part not only in instructing judges as to how to manage a caseload but also to assist in their re-education by encouraging them to reflect on their, perhaps newly conceived, future role.

The Authors

LORD NOLAN OF BRASTED b. 1928. Wadham College, Oxford. Middle Temple 1953. Judge of the High Court 1982–91. Lord Justice of Appeal 1991–93. Lord of Appeal in Ordinary 1994–. Chairman of Committee on Standards in Public Life 1994–.

SIR STEPHEN SEDLEY b. 1939. Queens' College, Cambridge. Inner Temple 1964. Judge of the High Court 1992–. Honorary Professor, University of Warwick 1994–.

PROFESSOR GEOFFREY WILSON b. 1930. Queens' College, Cambridge. Gray's Inn 1954. Fellow of Queens' College, Cambridge 1953–67. Lecturer in Law, University of Cambridge 1955–67. Founding Professor of the University of Warwick Law School 1967. Professor of Law, University of Warwick 1967–97.

Index

Persons whose views are discussed are included within the index. Persons merely mentioned, are not.